LIES AND LIARS

LIES AND LIARS

How and Why Sociopaths Lie and How You Can Detect and Deal with Them

by Gini Graham Scott, PhD

Skyhorse Publishing

Skyhorse Publishing books may be purchased in bulk at special discounts for
sales promotion, corporate gifts, fund-raising, or educational purposes. Special
editions can also be created to specifications. For details, contact the Special
Sales Department, Skyhorse Publishing, 307 West 36th Street, 11th Floor,
New York, NY 10018 or info@skyhorsepublishing.com.

Skyhorse® and Skyhorse Publishing® are registered trademarks of Skyhorse
Publishing, Inc.®, a Delaware corporation."

Visit our website at www.skyhorsepublishing.com.

10 9 8 7 6 5 4 3 2 1

Library of Congress Cataloging-in-Publication Data is available on file.

Cover design by Rain Saukas
Cover photo: iStockphoto

ISBN: 978-1-5107-6806-2
Ebook ISBN: 978-1-63450-388-4

Printed in the United States of America

CONTENTS

ABOUT THE AUTHOR

Gini Graham Scott has published over fifty books with mainstream publishers, focusing on social trends, work and business relationships, and personal and professional development. Some of these books include *Internet Book Piracy* (Allworth Press 2016), *Scammed* (Skyhorse Publishing 2016), *The New Middle Ages* (Nortia Press 2015), *Turn Your Dreams Into Reality* (Llewellyn 2015), *The Very Next New Thing* (ABC-Clio 2010), *The Talk Show Revolution* (ASJA Press 2008), *The Privacy Revolution* (ASJA Press 2008, previously published as *Mind Your Own Business: The Battle for Personal Privacy*, Plenum 1995), and *Fantasy Worlds* (ASJA Press 2007, previously published as *The Power of Fantasy*, Carol Publishing 1994).

Scott has gained extensive media interest for previous books, including appearances on *Good Morning America, Oprah, Montel Williams, CNN,* and hundreds of radio interviews. She has frequently been quoted by the media and has set up websites to promote her most recent books, featured at www.ginigrahamscott.com and www.changemakerspublishingandwriting.com.

She has become a regular Huffington Post blogger since December 2012 and has a Facebook page featuring her books and films at www.facebook.com/changemakerspublishing. Her articles and blogs about social issues and everyday life are also featured on her blog at www.ginigrahamscott.com/blog.

She has written, produced, and sometimes directed over sixty short videos, which are featured on her Changemakers Productions website at www.changemakersproductions.com and on YouTube at www.youtube.com/changemakersprod. Several recent short videos dealing with social issues are being pitched for development into full-length films. These include: *Forgive Our Taxes, The Middle Class Homeless, The Truth About Lying,* and *Internet Book Piracy.* Her full-length feature film *The Suicide Party #Save Dave* is being released in 2016; her second feature *Driver* is in production with Dear Skyyler Productions for release in 2017.

She has a PhD in sociology from U.C. Berkeley and MAs in Anthropology, Pop Culture and Lifestyles, Mass Communications and Organizational/Consumer/Audience Behavior, and Recreation and Tourism from Cal State, East Bay. She is working towards an additional MA there in Communications.

Additional bio and promotional material is at her websites at www.ginigrahamscott.com and www.changemakerspublishingandwriting.com.

INTRODUCTION

I hadn't intended to write a book about sociopathic liars. But after I spent two years living in L.A. to get into the film business, I found myself drawn into the web of a woman I'll call Sylvia who claimed she could produce and direct my script. She continually lied about it for five years, until I discovered the truth. At the same time, she victimized an associate, Rick, after she and her partner shot a film for him in another country and refused to give him the film. When he called me to declare Sylvia and her partner were criminals, she told me increasingly bizarre stories about Rick's connections to a criminal underworld that were after her and her partner, so she feared for her life and put the film under lock and key.

At the time, I believed her. How could someone who presented herself as a successful producer invent such stories? But in time, as explanations and excuses mounted about the delay in editing my film, I began to question and finally doubt her. When I spoke to others from the cast and crew, I uncovered an extensive pattern of secrets and lies, and I realized I had missed many warning signs along the way. I had become the victim of a sociopathic liar, as had my business associate and many cast and crew members.

This experience inspired my research into sociopathic liars, who are at the extreme end of a continuum of liars, and according to varying research accounts represent about 1–4 percent of the population. A higher perspective of sociopaths may be in certain fields, where there is pressure to gain success, so deception and trickery may be part of one's repertoire to achieve this end.

In 1994, I published a book called *The Truth About Lying* about how and why people lie and how to detect and deal with their lies. That book was inspired by several people lying to me in various business dealings, and in writing the book, I developed a Lie-Q Test to score people on the how much they lied. This led to a continuum of liars in four major categories—the self-proclaimed Model of Absolute Integrity who almost never lies, the Real Straight Shooter who normally doesn't lie, and the Pragmatic Fibber and Real Pinocchio, with a greater aptitude for lying. These four categories included almost everyone—and everyone lies—and for most people, lying was largely a practical way to get along in the world and have better relationships with others. Virtually no one was a compulsive or sociopathic liar.

After my book published, lying became even more common and acceptable after President Clinton put the face of a popular politician on everyday lying due to accusations about the Monica Lewinsky affair in 1998. Initially he protested "I did not have sex with THAT woman," though ultimately Clinton came clean and followed these revelations with an apology tour, which put him back in the nation's good graces. In turn, this saga of lying and forgiveness increased public awareness about lying and led to a new interest in lying, generally from books and articles about detecting lies and those revealing the extent of lying in public and political life.

Later, reality TV and game shows like *Survivor* and *Big Brother* helped to make lying not only acceptable but a necessary strategy to win the game through manipulating others and lying when necessary to remain on the show. The winning approach was lying strategically to create alliances while betraying others and offending the least number of people who might vote against one in the end.

Yet, while everyday lying has become more common and acceptable, there is a great distinction between pragmatic, socially acceptable lies and the big lies which become a crime and result in deep public scorn—as in the Bernie Madoff case, or the frequent and guiltless lies of a sociopath, which harm others. Such a sociopath is commonly charming and articulate, so it can be hard to detect the lies, which makes it more devastating when the lies are uncovered, after a close personal or long-term business relationship. These lies can be especially harmful when they lead unaware victims to actions based on these lies, such as by investing or loaning large sums of money based on false assurances and promises.

After an introductory discussion on the research findings about sociopaths, the book features interviews with sociopaths and victims with a focus on sociopaths who have been successful in everyday life.

To this end, the book covers the following topics:

- my personal experiences with lying
- understanding the reasons for lying
- the lies sociopathic liars tell in different situations
- the relationship of victims and sociopaths
- the experiences of victims who have lived or worked with sociopathic liars
- recognizing when someone is lying
- determining how to deal with a suspected or unmasked sociopathic liar.

PART I:

INTRODUCING THE LIES OF A SOCIOPATH

CHAPTER 1:
LIES AND DAMNED LIES IN L.A.

How could I miss all the signs that I was dealing with a sociopathic liar, when I came to L.A. with high hopes of getting some of my scripts produced as films? Many warning signs were flashing, but I wasn't aware of them since I was new to the industry and was new to the common behaviors and traits of a sociopath. Also, I naively wanted to trust and believe the best in others, though now I know to temper that approach with a more "show me" attitude. So by way of introduction, let this story serve as a cautionary tale for others.

I should have recognized the first warning sign, when I met Sylvia, who claimed to be a successful producer at a 2007 film funding conference in L.A. where she was promoting a new film. I had just been to a workshop on how to raise less than $20,000 for a microbudget film shot in minimal locations. After I had the money for such a film, Sylvia expressed interest in helping me, and we met at a coffee shop near the freeway when I drove from L.A. to Oakland, where I lived at the time.

Sylvia described being very successful in building a dozen health franchises to over $10 million in annual sales, although she claimed the company owner forced her out since he felt she was earning too much in commissions. So now she hoped to repeat this success in the film business. Moreover, she claimed she could call in some favors to make my low budget film look like a $200,000 film.

Though I was impressed, in hindsight, I came to recognize many warning signs, the first one being that Sylvia never mentioned the company by name. But knowing little about the film business, I accepted what Sylvia told me as true and I imagined that her huge success in this other business might indicate she could turn my small investment into a successful film. Yet her claims should have been a warning, since successful lies often don't include specifics one can check and verify. Plus sociopathic liars often embellish and exaggerate to show they are successful to persuade others to help them get what they want. And they may be eager to lie to place any blame for problems on others.

In any case, wooed by Sylvia's success claims, I agreed to move forward with her, and on my next trip to L.A. we worked out the agreement. Then again, I ignored any warning signs, including her persuading me to increase the budget to $40,000 with a $10,000 payment to herself, since she would be spending so much time on day-to-day production details. Still another warning sign was her telling me not to let anyone know about her $10,000 salary or the budget, since she would get about $200,000 in favors and make this look like a big budget film. Sylvia's "don't tell" requests were the beginning of a series of secrets and lies that are a common pattern for sociopaths, who create a web of lies to achieve their success.

A few months later, casting began. I didn't recognize still more warning signs, such as Sylvia's conflicts with the more experienced directors to whom I introduced her in order to guide her as a co-director, since she had no credit directing a film before. But repeatedly, Sylvia declared that these directors were not as experienced as they claimed. She also now claimed that she had been a director on a recent film she was promoting, but didn't get any credit because she made the film with her partner, who wanted full credit for himself and she gave it to him, supposedly because, "It's something you do for love," she said.

So again I accepted her explanation, although I should have been suspicious about her changing story, and eventually, she became the sole director of my film, though I should have seen her inability to get along with other directors as another warning, since sociopaths often disparage others or make false claims about their experience to make themselves look good.

More delays and excuses occurred: when we were in the midst of casting, she repeatedly claimed she was waiting for a cinematographer with a red camera to return from a film project abroad. But after six months when he allegedly returned, she said he had another job, and she needed to find another camera person, which took several more months.

Meanwhile, I referred a business associate, Jerry, to Sylvia's partner for a rewrite in return for a 10 percent referral fee. But that led to still more lies in which she disparaged Jerry as a pest who repeatedly called for advice, until she finally told him to stop calling, which I later discovered was part of a strategy to separate me from my associate—a divide and conquer strategy that sociopaths frequently use in power games.

There were more lies when Sylvia claimed she had to visit a sick sister back East, which I later discovered was a ruse to cover up a trip to film a documentary for Jerry for three weeks in Indonesia with her partner. But after she returned and casting of the film continued, the big reveal came a few months later, when Jerry called in a panic claiming that Sylvia and her partner were criminals (You'll read more about Jerry's story in Chapter 4.)

I was stunned. But when I was ready to cancel the project, Sylvia had a series of explanations after apologetically admitting the lie. Among them, she told me: "My partner didn't want me to tell you about the script, because he didn't want to pay the commission . . .I didn't give Jerry the film, because my partner and I wanted to edit it ourselves, since we feared Jerry would edit it very cheaply, which would hurt our reputations." In other words, she blamed the lies on her partner and Jerry, though I should have realized this attempt to blame others and not take responsibility herself was another warning sign.

To further convince me, Sylvia had several people contact me to say she was a good person and that I should forgive her for this one lapse. Only later did I find out that Sylvia had gotten an associate to make these calls or maybe she even did herself, since she was an actress. So she used a lie to get out of being caught in another lie, building an expanding edifice of lies to explain away previous lies when she had been caught.

Looking back, I realize I should have recognized her use of wilder and wilder lies to back up her story as a sign of a sociopath weaving an increasingly elaborate web of lies. But I didn't know what to look for at the time.

Over the next week, I went through a crisis of who to believe, though I should have recognized Sylvia's wild story as an even more elaborate lie. But she seemed so apologetic and sincere about wanting to make my film, even offering to take no more salary to repay me for the commission I should have gotten. Plus I had already paid her $7500, and she was starting to cast the film, which she still claimed would look like a million dollars because of all the favors she would get.

So now that the past lies were exposed and seemingly atoned for, albeit by the erroneous phone calls made to me, I thought she would continue on the project in a spirit of truth and forthrightness. But, boy, was I ever wrong, though I didn't realize this for over four years.

To make a long convoluted story short, among other things, Sylvia began to change the script on the set, including turning an agent from a supporting character into a lead to give her partner a leading role. And worse, she turned my suspense thriller about a wanna-be producer who goes on a revenge vendetta against a former mentee into a romantic comedy narrated by a dog. Why? Because she bought a puppy for a brief kidnap scene and later claimed this would be good for the film, since a Disney executive liked films with dogs (although she never actually spoke to a Disney executive). If nothing else, she had the sociopath's great skill of building a facade of lies to cover up preceding lies, and she told them in such a convincing way that they actually seemed very believable.

When it came time to edit the film, she delayed with more explanations, excuses, and reasons why she couldn't show me the film, such as claiming that a Russian editor with the original footage on his hard drive had to go overseas for a few months to work on a project, so she couldn't find another editor and had to wait for his return. But when he came back, he had another job. Another story was that she had put in $80,000 of her own money to finish the film, but no longer had any money to pay an editor. Then, she fell down an escalator, and was in a cast for six months. And when she gave someone $1,000 to get a loan, he disappeared, so she lost that money, and a prospective editor from her office proved unreliable. After about three years of this, when I offered to have someone in the Bay Area edit the film, now that I had written and produced forty short videos locally and knew more about what I was doing, she found an excuse to turn down my offer, claiming that she didn't want to give me the film, because she was afraid I would steal it from her and because she had to be with the editor to guide him. Again, I should have seen through her lies and confronted her, but I kept giving her the benefit of the doubt.

Meanwhile, as I became part of the Bay Area film community, I finally woke up and began to doubt Sylvia's excuses. At last I gave her an ultimatum to finish the film by the next American Film Market in November 2013 or return the money I paid and keep the film for herself.

That was the beginning of the end of what had been a long charade. Not surprisingly, I didn't hear from Sylvia again about the film—a disappearing act that often happens when sociopaths realize that they have been exposed and the game is up. Then, a month later, I discovered that Sylvia had posted online a trailer for her romantic comedy narrated by her dog under another title, so she was claiming my film as her own. And later I realized this was one more ploy of a sociopath—having no conscience about taking something away from someone or betraying to reach one's goal—in this case, recognition for directing her first film.

Eventually, after I wrote Sylvia a series of letters about breach of contract, copyright infringement, and a request to take down the trailer with no response, I sent a take-down notice to the website host who took it down. Since then, nearly a year later, neither the trailer nor the website have reappeared anywhere again. And later, when I contacted the cast and crew members from the set from five years before, and called Jerry to reestablish a connection, I discovered the many ways in which Sylvia had repeatedly lied to them too—including telling everyone that the line producer had left the film after five weeks because he embezzled from the film, when there was nothing to embezzle, and he had actually left because of health reasons and because he was tired of driving Sylvia around like a personal servant, because she had no car. She even told everyone she couldn't finish the film because I didn't give her any of that money that I had promised.

So the experience was an up close and personal look at how sociopaths operate, using lies to manipulate people to do what they want and separate people from each other, so they can't compare stories or work together.

Why didn't I recognize the signs sooner? Because that's the problem with dealing with a sociopath. Outwardly, they seem so normal, and are often very charming and articulate, so you don't suspect anything is wrong. And taken individually, the lies might seem reasonable, such as claiming an illness, accident, or delay because someone is out of town. Then, too, if you question anything, the sociopath always has a ready response, though it will most likely be another lie. And we commonly want to trust the people we are with, especially when they offer to do nice things for us or give us surprise gifts, such as when Sylvia brought me gifts from time to time. But gift giving is often part of a sociopath's charm to ingratiate him or herself, so a potential victim will more readily respond to their manipulations and accept their lies.

Also, reflecting the two-faced nature of the sociopath, Sylvia tried to be very helpful while trying to turn me against Jerry. For example, she did research on the Internet like a private investigator to find things to discredit him and show how little he knew about the film business.

So what can you do when you have suspicions that one has become a victim? In many cases, apart from ending the relationship, there isn't much you can do after the fact. The key to best dealing with a sociopath, as discussed, is to look for warning signs in the first place; then carefully disengage, so you don't become a victim of still more lies or a revenge vendetta for rejecting or exposing the sociopath.

In my own case, beyond sending out a take-down notice so Sylvia couldn't use any of the material I had paid for based on my copyrighted script and material, I found little I could do, as did Jerry when he tried to get back his film or the money he had paid Sylvia and her partner to make it. When we each spoke to the police, the officers told us the case sounded more like a civil matter, because any claims originated in a contract, and the lawyers we spoke to weren't willing to take the case on contingency. It would be an expensive case to pursue and it was uncertain if Sylvia or her partner had any money to collect. Also, the media would have little interest in the story, since Sylvia and her partner weren't famous, nor were we. Thus, sociopaths often can readily continue to do what they are doing, since after unraveling their web of lies and confronting them, one has little civil or criminal recourse. So they can easily go on to exploit the next victim.

Thus, I view my experience and that of my business associate as a cautionary tale with lessons on understanding how a sociopath operates in order to avoid being manipulated and victimized by a sociopath and their lies, while they may outwardly seem like a great friend, partner, or business associate.

I have written this book to make others aware of how the sociopath acts and lies, so readers can recognize the sociopaths in their lives and better deal with them. These sociopaths can be almost anyone—from a friend to a boss to a lover—and encountering and dealing with sociopaths is like traveling on a boat through shark-filled waters. You don't want to fall out, or let the shark climb in or destroy the boat.

CHAPTER 2:
THE LANGUAGE OF LYING

At its heart, lying is based on using statements, and actions supported by those statements, to mislead others to produce desired results—from getting money, jobs, position, and power to personal relationships and love. To this end, some lies may be told to facilitate everyday interactions, such as telling a white lie to feign interest and not hurt someone's feelings, or claiming to like something to smooth over a relationship. These are considered an acceptable, expected form of everyday lying. By contrast, more serious lies, if exposed, can undermine trust in a business or personal relationship, and liars may have to reinforce these lies with further details and explanations to make them credible.

Thus, lies exist on a continuum from everyday to more serious lies, while liars exist on a continuum from occasional to more frequent liars. The compulsive and sociopathic liars are at the extreme end, since they more frequently tell serious lies. They do so because lying becomes a habit for the compulsive liar and a way to achieve one's goals without them feeling any guilt or remorse. Thus, to better understand the compulsive and sociopathic liar and the types of lies they tell, it is important to understand about generally lying in everyday life.

The Pervasiveness of Lying

Lying actually is very common, since people deliberately deceive others to accept as true what the liar knows is false, in order to gain some benefit or avoid loss.[1] As numerous researchers have pointed out, people lie when a cost-benefit analysis fosters it, and they often get away with lying. Not getting caught encourages them to continue to do it, since most people have a truth bias, being predisposed to believe what they see and hear. So people are primed for being easily deceived. People also

---

[1] Sara Agosta, Patrizia Pezzoli, and Giuseppe Sartori. "How to Detect Deception in Everyday Life and the Reasons Underlying It." *Applied Cognitive Psychology*, 27 (2013) 256-262, p. 256.

expect to be told the truth under most circumstances. Our moral codes teach that lying is wrong, and this code is enforced by parents, teachers, and religious institutions. Even in the criminal justice system, a vow begins each trial with the promise to "tell the truth, the whole truth, and nothing but the truth." Indeed, society depends on the trust between individuals; it is part of the glue that holds personal relationships and society together.

Yet, in spite of all the strictures against it, lying is a very normal and common part of everyday human behavior, although some people—the compulsive and sociopathic liars—like far more than others. For example, one study of the US adult population by Kim Serota, Timothy Levine, and Franklin Booster found that the average person tells around 1.65 lies a day although most people claimed they told few or no lies each day, while a small percentage of liars were very prolific in telling untruths.[2]

Identifying the Lie: The Intention to Deceive

Central to the notion of lying is the intention to deceive the hearer to hold a false belief that something is true which the speaker believes is false. Thus, a lie is an insincere assertion.[3] While it usually is a statement of what is supposed to be true, it can also be a promise, which the liar does not intend to keep. Or a lie can be expressed through silence or a gesture implying agreement or acceptance of something, which the liar knows is untrue.

While the recipient of a communication may think something is a lie, because it misstates facts or because he or she believes the other person is intentionally providing wrong information, a false statement is not a lie without that intention. In that sense, a misstatement is simply an honest mistake by the person making the statement or a misperception by the person believing the statement to be a lie.

This distinction between a lie and a mistake is made for two related types of behavior that require an intention to deceive—cheating and stealing. It isn't cheating if a person doesn't know or understand the rules of a game or the social expectations for behavior. And it's not stealing when someone takes an item he believes he owns; it's just an accidental taking. But once a person has an intent to knowingly tell a falsehood, evade the

[2] Kim B. Serota, Timothy R. Levine, and Franklin J. Boster, "The Prevalence of Lying in America: Three Studies of Self-Reported Lies". *Human Communication Research*, 36 (2010) 2-25.

3 Jorg Meibauer, "On Lying: intentionality, implicature, and imprecision". *Intercultural Pragmatics*, 8 (2011) 277-292.

rules, or take something belonging to someone else without permission, he or she is guilty of lying, cheating, or stealing.[4]

In turn, any of these other behaviors, whether by intention, mistake, or accident, can be supported by lying, such as if a person claims he didn't know or understand the rules, when he did; or if a person says she didn't know the property belonged to someone else, when she knew it did. A person can also lie to support a lie, with a phony explanation or excuse rather than being caught telling a lie.

In some cases, engaging in an intentional fraud without guilt or remorse is a characteristic of the psychopath or sociopathic liar, who freely lies to justify any actions, including cheating, stealing, and telling lies.

Unfortunately, this need to show intention can make the lie very difficult to prove, especially since people want to believe in others' truthfulness and give them the benefit of the doubt. For example, in criminal law, many crimes by definition require *mens rea,* or the suspect knowingly having a general or specific intent to engage in a wrongful act. This requirement to show intent can sometimes make it difficult to prove a person was lying by knowingly making a false statement in a civil or criminal case involving a false statement or fraudulent act. Was the person mistaken due to misinformation? Or did the person *knowingly* lie? Any intention can be hard to prove, especially when an accomplished liar can quickly come up with reasons, explanations, and excuses to support the lie, as is commonly the case for the sociopathic liar.

Why the Lie?

There are dozens of reasons for lying, though usually, most people think of a lie as the outright fabrication of something which is presented as true or fact, with the person knowing he is presenting something as true when it is not.[5] By contrast, more commonly people tell half-truths, which contain some but not all true information, and they present what is true in a misleading way. Still another type of common lying is the omission or concealment of some important and relevant information, although some people don't consider not stating something to be telling a lie. But it is a lie, because it leads the other person to believe something that is untrue. Moreover, while people often don't realize this either, statements that assert a lie need not be verbal, since they can be made with gestures, nods, or silences that falsely imply an assent or disagreement with something someone else has said.[6]

---

[4] Ibid., p. 1597.
[5] Gini Graham Scott, *The Truth About Lying: Why and How We All Do It and What to Do About It,* Oakland, California: Changemakers Publishing and Writing, 2011, p. 4.
[6] Scott, p. 16.

Social lying can occur for everyone in everyday life. In fact, a series of research studies suggests that the average person tells at least .59 to 1.96 lies per day, while some people tell many more lies than others. For example, in "The Prevalence of Lying in America: Three Studies of Self-Reported Lies,'" Kim B. Serota, Timothy R. Levine, and Franklin J. Boster, found that many people claimed not to lie on a particular day. Though they do lie to others, most of the lies were told by a few prolific liars.[8] In other words, the researchers found that there is a mostly honest majority, while a small percentage of people lie a great deal. They also found that the frequent liars are likely to get away with it, because they appear to have a very honest demeanor.[9]

This observation about liars mirrored my own findings from a small survey using the Lie-Q test with about 100 people, in that the vast majority of people fell into the middle range with scores of 25–149 on a test where scores ranged from 0 to over 200 points.[10] Most people were honest most of the time or lied for a pragmatic reason. Only a very small percentage fell at the honest extreme of being a "model of absolute integrity," while only a small percentage were frequent liars. An even smaller group were compulsive or sociopathic liars who lied about almost everything.

Why the lie? In my book *The Truth About Lying: Why and How We All Do It and What to Do About It*, I identified a series of common reasons. Lies are sometimes told to help others, but mostly they are used to gain a personal benefit.[11] These include the following:

- sparing someone's feelings or making someone feel better
- gaining an advantage
- improving one's appearance
- getting out of an undesired activity or event
- appearing as more skilled or knowledgeable
- improving one's reputation
- hiding a mistake
- covering up something
- keeping a secret
- gaining a financial advantage or position in business

---

[7] Kim B. Serota, Timothy R. Levine, and Franklin J. Boster, "The Prevalence of Lying in America: Three Studies of Self-Reported Lies," *Human Communication Research*, 36 (2010), 2-25, p. 2.
[8] Serota, Levine, and Boster, p. 12.
[9] Ibid., p. 22.
[10] Scott, p. 206.
[11] Scott, p. 20.

- seeking revenge or hurting someone due to jealousy
- increasing one's self-esteem
- saving face or avoiding embarrassment
- getting someone to do something

And that's just some of the personal reasons for lying. Many other lies are told to protect others in a particular situation.

But despite the specific reasons for telling a lie, an underlying reason for all lying is that it is a form of self-defense. While commonly, lies are expressed to others through statements, non-verbal gestures, or actions to mislead, sometimes individuals lie to themselves, such as to deny a truth, because it would be too upsetting or too hurtful to acknowledge. Or in some cases, a self-lie can begin as a lie told to someone else, but as the person repeatedly tells that lie, he or she can come to believe it. An example is a lie to impress others, which a person comes to believe as true, so he or she no longer thinks it is a lie. So the lie turns into their reality, though it's still just a delusion.[12]

Lying in Different Situations

Lying for a wide range of reasons is thus widespread. One way to distinguish the different types of lies is by the situation. As described in *The Truth About Lying*,[13] these include:

- telling everyday social lies to smooth over relationships, such as by covering up real feelings and opinions to create a better image or avoid undesirable contact;
- lying to neighbors and others in public life, such as to feign interest or support;
- lying at work, such as to get a job or promotion, make excuses or cover up delays, obtain a goal, or get more money; lying in business, such as to take credit, make "can-do" claims when one can't do something, or to best a competitor;
- lying to friends and relatives;
- lying in playing the dating game;
- lying to husbands, wives, and intimate others;
- lying to children or parents;
- lying to oneself.

[12] Scott, p. 31.
[13] Scott, pp. ix-xi

Distinguishing Different Types of Lies

Besides distinguishing between lying in different situations, lies can be characterized based on content or context. For example, Bella De Paulo et. al,[14] point out that lies can be distinguished as:

- outright lies, where the information is entirely different or contradictory to what is true;
- exaggerations, in which a liar overstates or expands upon the truth to convey a false impression;
- subtle lies, based on the liar being evasive or omitting relevant information to mislead.

Moreover, lies can be distinguished in five different categories, based on their content, which include:

- feelings—lies about emotions, opinions, and evaluations, which include pretending to have feelings and assessments that are more or less positive than the truth;
- achievements and knowledge—lies to impress with more or greater accomplishments than are true and concealing the truth about failures, shortcomings, or a lack of knowledge;
- actions and plans—lies about what the liar has done, is doing, or plans to do;
- explanations—lies about reasons, explanations, or excuses for what the liar has or hasn't done;
- facts—lies that distort the truth about anything, including objects, events, people, and possessions.[15]

Other common distinctions are between lies told to benefit others or oneself and the real serious lies and white lies. Gray lies fall somewhere in the middle, and might be viewed as real or white lies depending on the circumstances.[16] As Eric Bryant points out, white lies are commonly viewed as benign, harmless, or acceptable lies, whereas real lies are considered harmful and unacceptable. While real lies are unacceptable violations of trust and are not very common, white lies are generally accepted and relatively common, since most people believe white lies are told to serve a greater good, such as being tactful in a social situation or making someone feel

---

[14] Bella M. DePaulo, et. al., "Lying in Everyday Life," *Journal of Personality and Social Psychology,* 1996, Vol. 70., No. 5, 979-995.

[15] Agosta, Pezzoli, and Sartori, p. 256.

[16] Eric Bryant, "Real Lies, White Lies and Gray Lies: Towards a Typology of Deception". *Kaleidoscope,* 7 (2008), 23-48.

better. As such, these lies are commonly thought of as "other-oriented" or "tactful lies," and often they are used to maintain a relationship, defer to a superior's authority, or protect the self-image of the person telling the lie."[17]

These white lies are so common, they often are not considered as lying but as "normal" behavior. In fact, people who can correctly tell such lies are said to have "communication competence", because these lies are regarded as a "social lubricant" to help create smooth social interactions.[18]

Still another way to think of lying is to imagine it to exist within a "norm of honesty," whereby there is an "acceptable range of dishonesty," i.e., individuals can behave dishonestly within this range without any negative consequences for lying.[19] Where is this range? It depends on the social context or culture as to what is acceptable lying. In some groups, such as in high society or political circles, politeness and tact are especially important, so evasiveness to smooth over social relationships may be perfectly acceptable. By contrast, while in other groups, based on friendship or other personal ties, frankness and openness is the norm.

In turn, as long as lying falls within the acceptable range, people may feel fine about lying, since they have the permission of their culture to be deceptive in order to be tactful, and certain constraints keep most people within that range. One common constraint is the fear of getting caught in a lie, so that one suffers shame or other negative consequences or punishments for lying. Another constraint is what researchers call "guilt aversion," in which people feel upset and remorseful if they violate their own moral dictates of what is right and wrong, so they feel guilty.[20] Because lying makes them feel guilty, they feel bad, so they may avoid telling a lie. But some liars accept feeling guilty for a time as the price for telling a lie, so they are willing to lie due to the potential for gain.

Other factors that influence lying are whether lying occurs in a non-personal or personal situation or whether an individual uses intuition or reason to decide if lying is acceptable under the circumstances. Another factor is whether one is in a business setting, where market considerations influence the choice to lie or not. For example, researchers have found that people lie less in personal relationships or about personal matters, and lie less when they rely on their intuition to make a moral judgment, rather than using their reasoning to consider the consequences of lying. By contrast, people are more apt to lie if they are influenced by financial considerations and benefits for telling the lies.[21]

---

[17] Bryant, p. 26.
[18] Bryant, p. 26.
[19] Argo and Shiv, p. 1095.
[20] Battigalli, Charness, and Dufwenberg, p. 228.
[21] Alexander W. Cappelen, Erik O. Sorensen, and Bertil Tungodden, "When do we lie?" *Journal of Economic Behavior & Organization*, 93 (2013), 258-265, p. 259.

Likewise, numerous researchers have found that "deception in inter-personal relationships is not only common but socially acceptable," so that it is viewed as a "normal" or ordinary part of interpersonal communication rather than a type of social or moral deviance.[22] In such relationships, the five major motivations for lying include: to save face with others and within oneself, to guide social interaction, to avoid tension or conflict, to influence interpersonal relationships, and to achieve interpersonal power. Or more generally, individuals may be motivated to lie to defend themselves socially or economically when in a disadvantaged situation, such as when someone lies to avoid being punished or fired for a mistake on the job.

By contrast, an individual is less likely to lie in a primary or close personal relationship, where bonds of trust are especially important and expected. They are also more likely to distort the truth in a non-inti-mate relationship, such as with a superior at work compared to a peer, frequently as a power-balancing strategy to provide a social or economic defense when they are at a disadvantage. [23] This impetus to lie in this situa-tion is much like the classic example of the little kid who is found grabbing cookies from the cookie jar and denies any culpability by responding: "I didn't take any cookies," as if the reality of taking cookies will go away by claiming it isn't so.

Researchers have additionally found that individuals may lie more if they interact more with others, since they have more opportunities to do so.[24] They may lie more, too, when asked to respond to a probing question or request, since they may feel on the spot to provide an answer. So they may lie for self-protection, much in keeping with the old saying: "Ask me no questions, and I'll tell you no lies." For example, a husband confronted by a wife who insistently asks, "Where have you been?" might lie because he doesn't want to admit he has stopped at a bar for a drink on his way home.

Personality and Telling Lies

Finally, some researchers have found a relationship between telling lies and personality types, suggesting that people with certain personality traits are more apt to lie or continue to do so. For instance, in "Individual Differences in Persistence in Lying and Experiences While Deceiving," Aldert Vrij and Michelle Holland found that the qualities associated with lying include social adroitness, public self-consciousness, other-directedness, emotional

---

[22] Paula V. Lippard, "Ask Me No Question, I'll Tell You No Lies: Situational Exigencies for Interpersonal Deception." *Western Journal of Speech Communication*, 52 (1988) 91-103, p. 91.

[23] Lippard, pp. 92, 99.

[24] Lippard, p. 99.

control, social control, acting, social expressivity, extraversion, and sociability.[25]

Such qualities are associated with lying for several reasons. Individuals who are socially adroit are more likely to lie frequently, since they are less concerned with conventional morality and are willing to manipulate others to get what they want. Those high in public self-consciousness are apt to lie to make a good impression on others. And people more skilled in controlling their emotional and social behavior can better employ impression management to tell a convincing lie, such as appearing outwardly calm, though inwardly upset. People skilled in impression management also have an ability to play roles and better present themselves to others; they are in essence good actors when they interact with others.

Likewise, those who are extraverted and sociable, so they enjoy interacting with others, are more confident in what they say and how others will react to them, so they can more confidently tell a lie. Conversely, people who are more reserved, shy, self-conscious, and socially anxious, are more likely to feel uncomfortable when lying. They fear giving off signals so others can tell they are lying, making them less apt to lie. As Vrij and Holland expected and found in their study, being manipulative, eager to make a good impression, and good at exercising control over verbal and non-verbal behaviors were positively related to persistence in lying.[26]

The Many Possibilities for Lying

The possibilities for lying are endless, and some liars find creative ways to conceal their lies, such as creating false personas and second lives. Another strategy to avoid being caught is to create lies on top of lies in the hope the subsequent lie will conceal or explain away the earlier lie.

Given the general disapproval of lying, commonly individuals find ways to justify their lie to themselves and others, especially when exposed in a lie they can't explain away to show they had a good reason for lying. In this way, they can continue to present themselves as a "good" person and quench any feelings of guilt which some feel for telling a lie.

The Continuum of Lying

Given this commonality of lying for many different reasons in different circumstances, sociopathic and compulsive liars are at the end of a

[25] Aldert Vrij and Michelle Holland, "Individual Differences in Persistence in Lying and Experiences While Deceiving." *Communications Research Repors*, 15 (1998), 299-308, pp. 300-301.
[26] Vrij and Holland, p. 305.

continuum in that they tell more serious lies more often. For them, lying becomes a habitual way of life, and commonly they are very good at lying, because they have been doing it for so long and have generally gained repeated benefits for themselves and sometimes for others with their lies.

The main difference between the sociopathic and compulsive liar is that the sociopath feels no guilt or remorse for lying, since he or she has no conscience and no concern with harming others with a lie. He or she lies as a pragmatic lifestyle choice, since it generally works well to gain various personal advantages. As a result, the sociopathic liar continues to lie frequently and well. By contrast, the compulsive liar lies due to inner personal demons, sometimes resulting from childhood experiences, that lead to their lying to relieve feelings of stress or gain attention or appreciation. However, some individuals are both: they are driven to compulsively lie due to psychological factors, and they become a sociopathic liar who repeatedly lies, without any feelings of guilt or concern for others, since they can achieve personal gains by doing so.

In short, compulsive or sociopathic liars lie for much the same reasons that other people lie, although they do so more frequently in more situations, and they more commonly tell the more serious lies out of habit or without remorse. In turn, their lies can be much more destructive, since they frequently breach the bonds of trust in a relationship as well as the norms of honesty, which lead others to unknowingly give them the benefit of the doubt.

Assessing Yourself and Others: What's Your Lie-Q?

So where do you fall on the continuum of lying? And where do others you know fall?

Here's a description of the test which I developed and initially included in my book *The Truth About Lying*.

QUIZ

What's Your Lie-Q?

(Lying Quotient)

*T*his simple quiz does not aspire to provide a serious scientific evaluation of your character in matters of lying. It does try, though-in an entertaining way-to make you aware of your propensity not to tell the truth in different situations of your personal, social, and professional life. Answer the questions *honestly*. Then add up the numbers in the circles corresponding to your answers and look up your score (on a scale of 0-285) on the key at the end of the quiz.

1. Give yourself the number of points indicated for your response to the following statements about lying.

   a. It is always wrong to tell a lie.   _____
       Yes   (0)
       No   (2)
       Not sure   (1)

   b. It is all right to lie, as long as the lie doesn't harm anyone.   _____
       Yes   (2)
       No   (0)
       Not sure   (1)

SUBTOTAL

c. It is never right to tell a lie that will harm anyone.   _____
       Yes   (0)
       No   (2)
       Not sure   (1)

d. It is all right to lie in order to protect oneself from harm.   _____
       Yes   (2)
       Yes, but only if it is   (1)
          really serious harm
       No   (0)
       Not sure   (1)

e. It is all right to lie to hurt someone else if that person has
    done something to hurt one.   _____
       Yes   (2)
       Yes, but only if that person has (1)
          done one very serious harm
       No   (0)
       Not sure   (1)

f. It is all right to lie in order to protect someone else from
    being hurt.   _____
       Yes   (2)
       Yes, but only if that person   (1)
          will be hurt very seriously
       No   (0)
       Not sure   (1)

g. It is all right to lie to become successful or gain an advan-
    tage, as long as no one else will be hurt by that lie.   _____
       Yes   (2)
       No   (0)
       Not sure   (1)

h. It is all right to lie to become successful or gain an advan-
    tage, because that's the way life is, and so it's necessary to
    do it.   _____
       Yes   (2)
       No   (0)
       Not sure   (1)

i. It is all right to lie when the benefit to be gained out-
    weighs the harm to result from that lie.   _____
       Yes   (2)
       No   (0)
       Not sure   (1)

SUBTOTAL   (_____)

2. What are the main reasons you would tell a lie? (Rate your biggest
   reasons with a 2; your occasional reasons with a 1; and reasons when
   you would never tell a lie with a 0.)

To protect someone from harm   (___ x 1=)_____
To cover up an embarrassing situation   (___ x 2=)_____
To avoid punishment   (___ x 2=)_____
To make someone feel good   (___ x 1=)_____
To get revenge   (___ x 3=)_____
To get a job   (___ x 1=)_____
To get a promotion   (___ x 2=)_____
To get more money   (___ x 2=)_____
To get out of an undesired social obligation   (___ x 1=)_____
To further your reputation   (___ x 1=)_____
To escape blame for a mistake   (___ x 2=)_____
To put the blame on someone else   (___ x 3=)_____
To conceal your age   (___ x 1=)_____
To seem more successful   (___ x 1=)_____
To do better on a test   (___ x 2=)_____
To obtain a contract   (___ x 2=)_____
To make a better deal in business   (___ x 2=)_____
To sell something to someone   (___ x 2=)_____
To pay less for something   (___ x 2=)_____
To have or cover up an affair   (___ x 3=)_____
To protect a member of your family   (___ x 1=)_____
To make someone you don't like look bad   (___ x 3=)_____
To hide an unpleasant truth about yourself   (___ x 2=)_____
To get out of paying a ticket   (___ x 2=)_____
To avoid being accused of something you did   (___ x 3=)_____
To cut through some bureaucracy more quickly   (___ x 1=)_____
To seem younger than you are   (___ x 1=)_____
To get ahead in line   (___ x 2=)_____
To get into someplace without paying   (___ x 2=)_____
To keep someone from knowing information
   they shouldn't know.   (___ x 2=)_____
To get a date   (___ x 1=)_____
To make the results of a project come out as desired(___ x 2=)_____
To keep someone from knowing something bad
   (e.g., an illness)   (___ x 1=)_____
To let someone think you like something
   when you don't   (___ x 1=)_____
To have a better sexual relationship (or to get sex)(___ x 2=)_____
To get out of doing something with someone
   you don't want to do something with   (___ x 2=)_____
To convince someone that your position is right   (___

SUBTOTAL   (_____)

3. Indicate on a scale of 0-3 how often you might lie to each of the following types of people. (0 = never; 1 = rarely; 2 = occasionally; 3 = often.)

salesmen	(_____ x 1= _____
customers or clients	(_____ x 2= _____
police officers	(_____ x 1= _____
clerks	(_____ x 1= _____
business associates	(_____ x 2= _____
employers	(_____ x 2= _____
employees	(_____ x 2= _____
friends	(_____ x 2= _____
relatives	(_____ x 2= _____
parents	(_____ x 3= _____
children	(_____ x 3= _____
neighbors	(_____ x 1= _____
priest/minister/rabbi	(_____ x 3= _____
lovers	(_____ x 3= _____
spouse	(_____ x 3= _____
pollsters	(_____ x 1= _____
reporters	(_____ x 1= _____
therapist/counselor	(_____ x 3= _____
teachers	(_____ x 2= _____
students	(_____ x 2= _____
business partners	(_____ x 3= _____

SUBTOTAL

4. How many lies have you told in the last week?

None	(0)
1-4	(1)
5-9	(2)
10 or more	(3)

5. How may lies have you told in the past day (or yesterday, if it's still early)?

None	(0)
1-4	(1)
3-4	(2)
5 or more	(3)

Now, total up your points from the five circles to get your Lie-Q! _____

Scoring Key

0-24 **A Model of Absolute Integrity** - but are you for real? You seem too honest to be believed.

25-49 **A Real Straight Shooter** - most of the time. Flexibly honest.

50-99 **A Pragmatic Fibber**

100-149 **A Real Pinocchio**

150-199 **A Compulsive Liar** - you probably cheated on this test.

200+ **Someone Who Will Lie about Almost Everything** - are you reading this in prison or on *Prime Time?*

CHAPTER 3:

UNDERSTANDING THE SOCIOPATHIC LIAR

Given the continuum of lying, compulsive and sociopathic liars generally are motivated to lie for the same reasons and in the same situations as other liars, although they lie more frequently, or as a habit, or without remorse. They also are more apt to lie under circumstances where others may not lie or where the norm of honesty is more expected, as in personal relationships. They also may tell bigger or more elaborate lies, and once caught in the cycle of lying, they may put more effort into building an edifice of lies, using more recent lies to protect earlier ones.

The major difference between the two types of liars is the psychological underpinnings that lead an individual to lie compulsively as a habit, compared to the sociopath's willingness to lie for personal gain without remorse for anyone who may be hurt by these lies. In many cases, the compulsive and sociopathic liar are one and the same, in that an individual both lies as a habit and feels no guilt or remorse. Much more research has been reported about the sociopathic, or psychopathic liar, the focus of this chapter. Though many psychologists make some distinctions, the term "sociopathic" is more commonly used than "psychopathic" to refer to both.

Understanding the Compulsive Liar

A compulsive liar is motivated to lie due to inner compulsions, so lying is often a symptom of certain psychiatric disorders, such as borderline personality disorder, bipolar disorder, or narcissism, although an individual may have developed this propensity to lie due to learning what worked as a child.[27]

These psychiatric disorders where lying is a symptom are widespread. According to Klaus Lieb and associates, about 1–2 percent of the general

---

[27] Parul Sharma, Ravi C. Sharma, Ramesh Kumar, and Dinesh D. Sharma, "Obsessive Compulsive Disorder with Pervasive Avoidance," *Indian Journal of Psychological Medicine*, 2009, Jul-Dec., 31(2), 101-103.

population is afflicted with a borderline personality disorder, which is characterized by a lack of impulse control, a rapid change of mood, a disturbed cognition, including suspicions and delusions, impulsive actions, and unstable relationships.[28] All of these characteristics can make a person more likely to lie.

In a bipolar disorder, which affects about 5 percent of the population, an individual experiences great mood swings, ranging from a deeply depressive to highly manic state, reflected in marked changes in self-perceptions of one's abilities and one's likely success.[29] In the manic state, an individual can feel a great sense of power and invincibility, and in the depressive phase, he or she can feel a sense of defeat and hopelessness. Such mood swings and perceptual changes can lead one to lie to feel better about oneself, or one might have grandiose, delusional ideas that lead to lies.

A narcissistic personality disorder, which affects about 6.2 percent of the population, can also contribute to a propensity to lie, since such individuals are generally highly self-absorbed and self-centered.[30] They typically have a high concern for personal adequacy, power, prestige, and vanity, so they might lie to build themselves up and look good to others.

Compulsive lying might arise as a symptom of one of these other disorders, since more than the average person, the compulsive liar finds it easy to lie, gains comfort in lying, and often lies when presented with the truth. Often he or she finds it more reassuring to support the lie and deny the truth.[31]

Compulsive liars often have an underlying psychiatric disorder or addiction, since many psychiatrists consider excessive lying a common symptom of a mental illness.[32] That's because the illness takes over rational judgment and leads to delusions and fantasies, as well as distorting relationships with other people. For instance, people who suffer from antisocial personality disorder use lying to exploit others, while some individuals with borderline personality disorder lie for attention by claiming poor treatment.

[28] Klaus Lieb, Mary C. Zanarini, Christian Schmahl, Marsha M. Linehan, and Martin Bohus, "Borderline Personality Disorder," *The Lancet*, Vol. 364, July 31, 2004, 454-461, p. 453.

[29] Christina Colombo, Andrea Fossati, and Francesc Colom, "Bipolar Disorder," *Depression and Treatment*, Vol: 2012, 1-2, p. 1. http://www.hindawi.com/journals/drt/2012/525837/

[30] Sebastien Larochelle, "Handbook of Narcissism and Narcissistic Personality Disorder: Book Review," *Canadian Psychology*, Vol 53, Issue 1 (31 January 2012), pp. 71-72.

[31] Kathleen Esposito, "Compulsive Lying Disorder," http://addiction.lovetoknow.com/wiki/Compulsive_Lying_Disorder

[32] Dike, C., Baranoski, M., & Griffith, E. (2005). "Pathological lying revisited." *The Journal Of The American Academy Of Psychiatry And The Law*, 33(3), 342–349. Retrieved from EBSCOhost

However, not all compulsive liars suffer from a psychiatric illness. They commonly lie to gain admiration, popularity, control, and the ability to manipulate others to compensate for low self-esteem. They seek to disguise failure by making others feel responsible or by casting the blame on someone else. [33]

Given this innate compulsion to lie from habit due to an underlying psychological disorder, the compulsive liar may not always lie effectively, since this compulsion may lead to lying for release rather for strategic reasons. So he or she is more likely to be caught in a lie. The compulsive liar is also apt to be less successful in life and to use lies as a self-delusion to create a fantasy life as a personal armor. So such a liar is more likely to alienate family members, relatives, friends, and others by their frequent lies, or to be subjected to psychological intervention or institutionalization to break the internal triggers for lying. Unfortunately, without treating these inner dynamics, it can be very difficult to stop the compulsive liar.

Thus, with many compulsive liars, it can be necessary to treat the inner illness to stop the lying, though outwardly, the compulsive liar's frequent and grandiose lies may appear the same as the lies of the sociopath, who lies for a personal benefit without feelings of empathy, guilt, or remorse.

Understanding the Sociopathic Liar

In contrast to the compulsive liar, the sociopathic liar commonly is good at lying, since he or she conceals the lies under a veneer of charm and an ability to quickly craft explanations to deflect any suspicions that they may be lying. The sociopath is used to getting away with lies, since most people, who only lie occasionally or rarely, tend to think that others are like themselves in being honest most of the time. So they tend to be readily sucked in by the sociopath's lies. Even one sociopath might not detect the lies of another, so two sociopaths might readily lie to each other as long as it is in their best interest to continue the personal or business relationship.

The difference between the sociopathic and compulsive liar is that the sociopathic liar will lie for absolutely no reason and do so very convincingly. They may lie at times to see if they can trick people, and they are good at lying in all types of circumstances because they lack any empathy for others, though commonly they lie to gain something. Their lying is usually calculated and cunning, and ultimately, someone is likely to get hurt, since the sociopath doesn't care who their lies will affect, as long as

[33] Kathleen Esposito, "Compulsive Lying Disorder," Love to Know Recovery, addiction. lovetoknow.com/wiki/Compulsive_Lying_Disorder.

their lies help them get what they want.[34] While they recognize the difference between right and wrong and realize that lying is wrong, they don't care. They may even come to believe their own lies.

In effect, the sociopath uses lying as a weapon to gain trust, sympathy, and pity from those to whom they lie, such as by telling a story that seems personally revealing or describes facing difficulties and hardship. While the story they tell (but embellish) often contains a grain of truth, in other cases they fabricate an entirely new reality. For instance, they might describe experiencing an abusive childhood or a series of accidents or illnesses to make the average person sympathetic to their plight and thus more willing to accept repeated excuses for their behavior.[35]

All the explanations, excuses, and more lies can sometimes help the sociopath avoid being caught in a lie, though sometimes multiple lies to many different people can trip them up, such as when they tell different versions of the same lie, and the people they lie to could become suspicious on comparing stories. They might also get caught when they reveal contradictions while telling the same story, since they may not remember what they said before to someone. But then, to protect themselves against suspicions and revelations, they may be vague on the details or take steps to make sure the various people to whom they tell different stories do not meet or compare stories; for example cooking up a reason to alienate former friends and associates from each other, so they don't share their experiences and discover the lies.

In a way, it is as if sociopaths have turned human relationships into a game, in which they do whatever it takes to win. It doesn't matter if they trample over other peoples' feelings, because they do not care about others. They have no empathy; no capability or desire to care about other people. No one is special to them unless they serve an immediate and necessary purpose.

The Characteristics of the Sociopathic Liar

The propensity to lie, along with other characteristics like the ability to charm and manipulate, are part of a list of common characteristics of the sociopath, once called the psychopath, according to a classic book from 1941, *The Mark of Sanity, An Attempt to Clarify Some Issues About the So-Called Pscyhopathic Personality,* written by Dr. Hervey Cleckley, an American psychiatrist. He developed a list of sixteen traits and behaviors of the psychopath based on his practice, and he later examined this

---

[34] Virtual Treasures, "Sociopathic Lying Tendencies—The Sociopath as a Pathological Liar," virtualtreasures.hubpages.com/hub/Sociopathic-Tendencies-Pathological-Lying

[35] Virtual Treasures, "Sociopathic Lying Tendencies—The Sociopath as a Pathological Liar," virtualtreasures.hubpages.com/hub/Sociopathic-Tendencies-Pathological-Lying

personality type in a variety of occupations and industries, including business, science, politics, medicine, and psychiatry. Later, Robert Hare, who studied the psychopath for many years, drew on Cleckley's list in creating the Psychopathy Checklist-Revised (PCL-R), now the most widely known instrument in assessing psychopathy.[36]

In his classic study, Cleckley divided the sixteen characteristics into interpersonal, affective, and behavioral characteristics. Interpersonally, he identified psychopaths as being "intelligent, egocentric, glib, superficially charming, verbally facile, and manipulative." Emotionally, he characterized them as individuals who "displayed short-lived emotions" and lacked important human qualities, such as "empathy and remorse." Behaviorally, he described them as "irresponsible, prone to seek novelty and excitation, and likely to engage in moral transgressions, antisocial acts, or both."[37]

Building on Cleckley's list, in 1991 Hare developed a model in which he separated the characteristics of the psychopath into two components— Factor 1 (F_1) representing the interpersonal and affective qualities, and Factor 2 (F_2) representing the behavioral aspects of the disorder. Between 2000 to 2004, several other researchers conducted factor analysis studies with adults and adolescents, which led to creating a three-factor structure to characterize the psychopath. In this system, the first factor reflects an arrogant and deceptive interpersonal style (known for short as ADI), the second factor reflects affective deficiencies or callous and unemotional traits (known as DAE) and the third factor reflects irresponsible and impulsive behavior (IIB).

When applied to children the three factors are called "Narcissism," "Callous-Unemotional Traits," and "Impulsivity," since researchers have found that these qualities commonly develop in childhood.[38]

Researchers have also found that psychopathy and intelligence are related, since the psychopath has excellent rational powers and an above average or superior intelligence. Such intelligence, in turn, helps the psychopath con and manipulate others, charm others to advance their personal interests, and be composed and poised in social settings. In particular, the psychopath is likely to have good verbal skills and creativity, which contribute to his or her charm, manipulation, and ability to deceive.[39] If these traits sound like someone you know or seem to characterize people in

---

[36]   Katherine Ramsland, "Crystallizing Psychotherapy: Dr. Hervey Cleckley," *The Forensic Examiner,* Summer 2013, 62-65, p. 62.

[37]   Randall T. Salekin, Chair S. Neumann, Anne-Marie R. Leistico, and Alecia A. Zalot, "Psychopathy in Youth and Intelligence: An Investigation of Cleckley's Hypothesis," *Journal of Clinical Child and Adolescent Psychology,* 2004, Vol. 33, No. 4, 731-742, p. 731.

[38]   Salekin, et. al., p. 732-33

[39]   Salekin, et. al., p. 733.

certain fields, such as politicians and salesmen, well, that's why there are more sociopaths in certain fields, where being personable and charming while seeking success pays off.

Although Cleckley is still the major source for defining the nature of psychopathy, around 1980, American clinicians and other researchers focused on the behavior manifestations, and the name of the disorder began changing. In America, psychopathy got subsumed into the broader antisocial personality disorder category (also known as ASPD or APD) in *The Diagnostic and Statistical Manual of Mental Disorders (DSM)*, which psychiatrists use to identify different psychological disorders. However, researchers in other countries continued to use the PCL-R or other psychopathy assessments to identify the disorder, since they feel psychopathy should stand on its own.[40]

After all this debate among psychologists and psychiatrists, the disorder—or at least its major characteristics—came to be known in 1952 by the "sociopath" term still in common use today, although it has been referred to by other terms, such as being called one of the "sociopathic personality disorders" or a "personality disorder, antisocial type." In fact, some of the modern disputes and confusion about the term can be traced back to the nineteenth century, when "psychopathy" was the first personality disorder recognized in psychiatry. Initially, the term referred to a range of personality disorders that were considered extreme forms of the normal personality, and over the years a number of clearly pejorative terms were used, including "moral insanity, moral imbecility, degenerate constitution, congenital delinquency, constitutional inferiority, and psychopathic taint." But finally in the early twentieth century, the disorder was called by the more modern references: psychopathic personality, psychopathy, sociopathy, and more recently "antisocial personality disorder" and "dissocial personality disorder."[41]

One reason for these recent changes in terminology since the 1990s has been the trend to look at behaviors rather than personality characteristics. That's because it is relatively easy to observe and measure behaviors, rather than trying to identify personality traits, which are subjective and elusive.

As for the classic description by Cleckley, still used today, here's his list from the *Mask of Sanity*, drawn from the psychological literature and his clinical practice:

1.   Superficial charm and good intelligence
2.   Absence of delusions and other signs of irrational thinking
3.   Absence of "nervousness" or psychoneurotic manifestations
4.   Unreliability

---

[40] Ramsland, p. 64.

[41] James R. P. Ogloff, "Psychopathy/Antisocial Personality Disorder Conundrum," *Australian and New Zealand Journal of Psychiatry*, 2006; 40:519-528, pp. 520-521.

5. Untruthfulness and insincerity
6. Lack of remorse or shame
7. Inadequately motivated antisocial behavior
8. Poor judgment and failure to learn from experience
9. Pathological egocentricity and incapacity for love
10. General poverty in major affective reactions
11. Specific loss of insight
12. Unresponsiveness in general interpersonal relations
13. Fantastic and uninviting behavior, with drink and sometimes without
14. Suicide rarely carried out
15. Sex life impersonal, trivial, and poorly integrated
16. Failure to follow any life plan.[42]

Building on this list, Hare developed the Psychopathy Checklist Revised (PCL-R), to operationalize the characteristics of the psychopath using the interpersonal/affective and social deviance measures divided into two facets with these traits[43]:

Factor 1—Interpersonal/Affective
    Facet 1—Interpersonal
        • Glibness/Superficial Charm
        • Grandiose Self-Worth
        • Pathological Lying
        • Conning/Manipulative
    Facet 2—Affective
        • Lack of Remorse or Guilt
        • Shallow Affect
        • Callous/Lack of Empathy
        • Failure to Accept Responsibility for Actions
Factor 2—Social Deviance
    Facet 1—Lifestyle
        • Need for Stimulation, Prone to Boredom
        • Parasitic Lifestyle
        • Lack of Realistic, Long-Term Goals
        • Impulsivity
        • Irresponsibility
    Facet 2—Antisocial
        • Poor Behavioral Controls
        • Early Behavior Problems
        • Juvenile Delinquency

[42] Ogloff, p. 520.
[43] Ogloff, p. 522.

- Revocation of Conditional Release
- Criminal Versatility

While some of these antisocial traits were developed from study-ing juvenile delinquents and incarcerated criminals and may not apply to all psychopaths or sociopaths, over 100 peer-reviewed studies have supported the PCL-R's reliability and validity. Based on these measures, approximately 3–5 percent of the general population have an Antisocial Pathological Disorder, and about 1 percent have enough characteristics of the psychopath to score of 30/40 or more on the PCL-R.[44]

Studying the Sociopath

There are hundreds of studies about sociopaths, most using the older terms "psychopath" or "antisocial personality disorder," to better understand the relationship of this disorder to other personality traits and behaviors.

For example, Robert D. Hare, the psychology professor at the University of British Columbia in Vancouver, Canada, who developed the Hare Psychopathy Checklist, found that high scores were characterized by an early appearance of antisocial behavior, rather than with the psychological qualities usually associated with being a psychopath, such as a lack of empathy, guilt, remorse, or concern for others.[45] Thus, while some sociopaths might be drawn to engage in criminal behaviors or become psychotic, most others may not.

Later, David J. Cook and Christine Michie agreed that the interpersonal/affective Factor 1 items, such as having a lack of empathy, inflated self-ap-praisal, and superficial charm, were the most important indicators for diag-nosing the disorder.[46] Then, they further suggested that the disorder is due to three major factors—biological vulnerability, critical early experiences, and social pressures, although some traits might be triggered by social conditions, such as socioeconomic status, educational attainment, and family of origin.[47]

Still other researchers have found that individuals with the character-istics of a sociopath are more likely to commit fraud-like offenses, since sociopaths are prone to deceive and manipulate others. They also tend to be superficially charming, convincing, and verbally facile, while underneath they are callous, unreliable, unable to learn from experience, and wear a mask of sanity that covers their lack of feelings.[48] This makes the sociopath

[44] Ogloff, p. 524.
[45] Hare, p. 41.
[46] Cooke and Michie, p. 11.
[47] Cooke and Michie, p. 12.
[48] Jaana Haapasalo, "Types of Offense Among the Cleckley Psychopaths," *International Journal of Offender Therapy and Comparative Criminology*, 38(1), 1994, 59-67, p. 60.

better able to lie and successfully carry out fraudulent schemes, as Jaana Haapasol found in research at the University of Montreal in Canada.[49] After assessing the personality of ninety-two offenders convicted for property crimes, narcotics, and traffic offenses, she found that the psychopaths were convicted for more fraud-like offenses than the other offenders.[50]

Still other researchers have also found the strongest connection between having Factor 2 impulsive and antisocial behavioral traits and engaging in future antisocial conduct.[51]

Others have found a strong relationship between being a sociopath and intelligence. For example, Peter Johansson and Margaret Kerr at Orebro University in Sweden found this (i.e., the relationship between sociopath/ intelligence mentioned in previous sentence) after studying 370 men at a Swedish assessment center who were sentenced for four years to life for violent but nonsexual crimes. They discovered that the sociopaths with a higher total IQ and a higher verbal intelligence got an earlier start in violent crime. So they concluded that high intelligence seemed to make people with psychopathic personality traits more destructive, perhaps because they couldn't succeed as people with high intellectual abilities normally do: they were very impulsive and irresponsible, which undermined their ability to succeed. With the pathways usually open to people with superior intelligence closed to them, the sociopath might turn to a criminal career to express their potential.[52]

Paradoxically, these research studies are primarily conducted with prison inmates, hospital patients, and university students, yet the criteria that Cleckley and Hare first developed to identify the sociopath is still applied in popular magazine, books, and Internet advice on recognizing and dealing with a psychopath or sociopath.

Defining the Sociopath: A History of the Term

While contemporary conceptualizations of sociotherapy can be traced back to Cleckley's original characterization of the psychopathy syndrome,[53]

[49] Haapasalo, p. 59.

[50] Haapasalo, p. 66.

[51] Anne-Marie R. Leistico, Randall T. Salekin, Jamie DeCoster, and Richard Rogers, "A Large-Scale Meta-Analysis Relating the Hare Measures of Psychopathy to Antisocial Conduct." *Law and Human Behavior* (2008) 32:28-45, pp. 28, 31, 38-39. https://www. researchgate.net/publication/6207997_A_meta-analysis_relating_the_Hare_measures_ of_psychopathy_to_antisocial_conduct_Law_and_Human_Behavior_32_28-45

[52] Peter Johansson and Margaret Kerr, "Psychopathy and Intelligence: A Second Look," *Journal of Personality Disorders*, 19(4), 357-369 (2005), pp. 359, 366-367.

[53] Elwood, Poythress, and Douglas, pp. 833-834.

there is still a great deal of confusion over what to call the syndrome and what combination of traits to include.

The history of the syndrome goes back to 1801, when Phillipe Penel, a French doctor, observed that some of his patients engaged in impulsive acts, had episodes of extreme violence, and caused self-harm. He characterized them as suffering from *manie sans delire*, meaning insanity without delirium. [54]

Then, in 1835, the syndrome became known as "moral insanity," a term coined by J. C. Prichard, a British physician. He considered the syndrome "a morbid perversion of the natural feelings, affections, habits, moral disposition, and natural impulses," although the individual had no defect of intellect or reasoning. Even though these individuals knew the difference between right and wrong, the individuals engaged in bad behavior anyway.[55]

Later in 1897, H. Maudsley, a British psychiatrist, used the term "moral imbecility" to characterize convicts who couldn't control their actions and couldn't be reformed, because they had a "defective physical and mental organization."[56]

In 1915, a German psychiatrist, Emil Kraepelin ,who wrote the *Encyclopedia of Psychology* and is thereby called the founder of modern psychiatry, claimed that individuals with a "psychopathic inferiority" fall into four key personality types:

- the born criminal;
- criminals by impulse, who experienced uncontrollable desires to commit offenses regardless of whether they would achieve a material gain;
- professional criminals, who acted out of a "cold, calculated self-interest," rather than an uncontrollable impulse; and
- "morbid vagabonds, who wandered through life with neither self-confidence nor responsibility."[57]

The next big milestone came when Cleckley's 1941 breakthrough book, *The Mask of Sanity* was published. This marked the beginning of the modern clinical construct of psychopathy, though now the term "sociopath" is commonly used by both laypersons and mental health professionals. This popularization of the concept has resulted in a more accurate

---

[54]   Bruce A. Arrigo and Stacey Shipley, "The Confusion over Psychopathy (II): Historical Considerations," *International Journal of Offender Therapy and Comparative Criminology*, 2001 45:325-344, pp. 327, 330.

[55]   Arrigo and Shipley, p. 331.

[56]   Arrigo and Shipley, p. 332-333.

[57]   Arrigo and Shipley, p. 333.

characterization of the sociopath, since Cleckley and other researchers found that many psychopaths never got involved with the criminal justice system and non-offenders can be very successful in various occupations, especially in those that offer an opportunity for material success, such as business.[58]

According to Hare and Hare,[59] the sociopath developed their characteristic trait of not having a conscience due to a failure in the learning process and by the diminishing of normal human emotions, so that normally socializing experiences don't work with psychopaths.[60]

A decade later, in 1952, Cleckley's formulation underwent its first modern-day transformations, when the American Psychiatric Association published its first Diagnostic and Statistical Manual of Mental Disorders, commonly known as the DSM. For the first time, the DSM used the term "sociopath," when it renamed the psychopathic construct the "Sociopathic Personality Disturbance." This new term was designed to combine previous psychiatric explanation with more "socially sensitive interpretations" of the disorder[61] by considering the social and cultural factors which contribute to psychopathy. This first DSM also distinguished between the psychopath, characterized by antisocial behaviors (the antisocial psychopath), and the dissocial sociopath, who was a professional criminal, such as a member of organized crime, who could be very loyal to his associates.[62]

While the first and second DSM used the term "sociopath," subsequent DSMs used different terms and combined this initial construct into other psychiatric categories, though the "sociopath" term gradually became part of ordinary usage. However, the behaviors listed in this new approach were so broad they could include almost every known criminal offense.[63] In fact, a person needed to fall into only 4 out of 10 behavioral categories to be diagnosed with an Antisocial Personality Disorder, so literally anyone could be diagnosed this way. For example, if you look at the categories, you might easily find yourself there, such as if you have an inability to sustain consistent work behavior; fail to conform to social norms required for lawful behavior; are irritable and aggressive, take part in physical fights and assaults; engage in lying or impulsive conduct; have an inability to establish lasting, stable relationships; and have a disregard

---

[58] Arrigo and Shipley, pp. 333-334.

[59] S. D. Hare and R. D. Hare, "Psychopathy: Assessment and Association with Criminal Conduct," in D. M. Stuff, J. Breiling, and J. D. Maser (Eds), *Handbook of Antisocial Behavior*, New York: Wiley, 1997, 22-35.

[60] Arrigo and Shipley, p. 334.

[61] Arrigo and Shipley, p. 336.

[62] Arrigo and Shipley, p. 336.

[63] Arrigo and Shipley, p. 337.

for personal safety[64]—climbing mountains or going hang gliding come immediately to mind. Unfortunately, most people might engage in some of these behaviors at some time, making an ASPD diagnosis potentially applicable to anyone.

But finally Hare's PCL and PCL-R came to the rescue with his two factor analysis to identify the psychopath or sociopath. As noted, he used Factor 1 to describe the characteristic personality traits, such as glibness, superficial charm, a grandiose sense of self-worth, pathological lying, conning and manipulative behavior, a lack of remorse, shallow affect, a callous lack of empathy, and a failure to accept responsibility for one's actions. Then, he used Factor 2 to determine if the individual has the characteristic behavioral patterns, such as a proneness to boredom, a parasitic lifestyle, poor behavior controls, early behavioral problems, a lack of realistic long-term goals, impulsivity, and irresponsibility.[65]

The advantage of Hare's approach is that it takes both traits and behaviors into consideration to define the sociopath, although properly determining whether someone is or isn't a sociopath is still a big problem. Another problem is that it is virtually impossible to treat the sociopath, because since they are so good at lying and manipulation, they elude detection. Then, too, even if the assessment tools can identify the sociopath, such individuals are largely untreatable, given their lack of remorse, cunning, and ability to manipulate others. In fact, their ability at impression management and malingering can enable them to cheat any interview or test. By detecting the information sought, they give the needed impression or information.[66]

However, while most research on sociopaths has come from patients and prisoners, Joseph P. Cangemia and William Pfohl point out in "Sociopaths in High Places," based on their case studies and Martha Stout's book *The Sociopath Next Door*, that many sociopaths are actually very successful, high performers. They point out that sociopathic personalities can be very successful in a leadership role, as were seven individuals they studied in the industrial, academic, and non-profit organization world. These individuals achieved success by using their ability to manipulate others, along with their callousness, focused behavior, desire to destroy a competitor, delight in inflicting damage on another, and a remorseless willingness to do what it took, even if unethical, immoral, or illegal to get what they wanted.[67]

---

[64] Arrigo and Shipley, p. 337-338.

[65] Arrigo and Shipley, pp. 339-340.

[66] Arrigo and Shipley, pp. 414, 417.

[67] Joseph P. Cangemi and William Pfohl, "Sociopaths in High Places," *Organization Development Journal*, 27 (2009) 85-96, pp. 85, 95.

Thus, in spite of all the infighting by psychologists, psychiatrists, and academic researchers, the psychopath/sociopath construct has come to include certain key personality and behavioral traits. After first being used in the 1952 DSM, the term "sociopath" has more recently replaced "psychopath" in common usage. Over the decades, the characteristics and terms describing this syndrome have changed, but the classic definition derives from the work of Cleckley and further developed by Hare remains.

The Differences in the Way Sociopaths Lie

Though virtually everyone lies at some point—from lies to be polite and help others to lies to conceal something negative, or achieve a goal—the lies of sociopaths are qualitatively different. That's because, as discussed by Martha Stout in *The Sociopath Next Door*[68] and Robert D. Hare, the author of *Without Conscience,* [69] (who developed the classic PCLR scale used to identify sociopaths), sociopaths lack a conscience and an emotional attachment to others. So besides the ordinary lies that everyone tells, they can be more devious and destructive, because they don't care if they hurt someone. As a result, they can freely control and manipulate others at will to get what they want, limited only by a concern with the consequences of being caught. Then, they'll just lie to get out of being caught or to escape or mitigate the consequences if found out. As a result, they adopt a mask through their charm and lies, seemingly to show that they care, when that is all part of the show to achieve their goals. Without the emotional connection to others, life becomes a kind of game in which their main driving force is to win at any cost. So lies become one more means to get to this end.

As Stout points out: "Conscience propels us outward in the direction of other.people, toward conscious action both minor and great."[70] But since sociopaths lack this conscience and emotional attachment to others, they are free to do whatever they want if they can They'll use lies to achieve their end to get ahead and win, since that's what matters most to sociopaths, because they lack the emotional bonds towards others, along with lacking a conscience resulting from those bonds.

The Traits of a Sociopath

Some research has found exactly that—sociopaths in certain positions. For example, Kevin Dutton, author of *The Wisdom of Psychopaths*, conducted an online study using the Great British Psychopath Survey.

---

[68] Martha Stout, *The Sociopath Next Door*, New York: Harmony, 2005.
[69] Robert D. Hare, *Without Conscience*, New York: The Guildford Press, 1993.
[70] Stout, pp. 33, 35.

They found that individuals with high scores were in professions requiring good leadership and people skills—two of the traits in which successful sociopaths do well. Among these top ten professions were CEO, lawyer, media personality, salesperson, surgeon, journalist, police officer, clergyperson, chef, and civil servant. By contrast, the professions where individuals had low scores were characterized by traits like offering care, compassion and help to others, (such as being a care aide, nurse, therapist, beautician/stylist, charity worker, teacher, or doctor), or doing work that didn't involve people skills, (such as being a craftsperson, creative artist, or accountant[71]).

Such research results help to show that high functioning sociopaths might do quite well with a certain mix of characteristics, such as the qualities of ruthlessness, mental toughness, charisma, focus, persuasiveness, and coolness under pressure, which contribute to the ability to get ahead.[72] So it's no wonder that CEOs, salespeople, lawyers, media personalities, and others listed at the top of the traits of a psychopath do well. They have been able to control their qualities and put them to good use, unlike those with these qualities who turn to crime. Or as Joe Newman, a University of Wisconsin psychology professor explains, the combination of low risk aversion and the lack of guilt or remorse which are "two central pillars of psychopathy . . .may lead, depending on circumstances, to a successful career in either crime or business. Sometimes both."[73]

Yet, while sociopaths may not feel emotions themselves, they are able to mask that lack of feeling in the way they appear to others and can recognize emotions in others. In fact, that's what makes them so effective in sales and in being able to detect the vulnerability in potential victims, much like a predator can detect fear in its prey.

They also have a greater ability to focus, as well as to break away from social conventions, which may prove to be an advantage under some circumstances. For example, in one study on lying, psychologist Stephen Porter and his colleagues found that participants exhibiting higher levels of psychopathy were not only better at disguising their real feelings by feigning the opposite emotion when they looked at happy and sad images, but they were better able to detect deception by others. [74] They seem to know what best to say to exercise this control, since they can sense the victim's vulnerability and how to best tap into that, much like a master salesman might sense all the hot buttons to push to lead to a sale.

---

[71]   Kevin Dutton, The Wisdom of Psychopaths: What Saints, Spies, and Serial Killers Can Teach Us About Success, Farrar, Straus and Giroux, 2012, pp. 161-162

[72]   Ibid., p. 60.

[73]   Ibid., pp. 62-63.

[74]   Ibid., pp. 112-113, 119.

While researchers have found that conformity is the natural response for most people as a result of evolution, sociopaths may have an advantage in being able to break free of social convention and think outside the group, so they can make better decisions and life choices than most others who are swayed by the tendency to conform and go along with the thinking of the group.[75] Then, too, their relatively low level of anxiety may give them an advantage in enabling them to make more measured, rational decisions.[76]

Still other research has shown that men with certain key personality traits, including the self-esteem of narcissism; the fearlessness, ruthlessness, impulsivity, and thrill-seeking of psychopathy; and the deceitfulness and exploitiveness of Machiavellianismdo very well in certain spheres of society, according to psychologist Peter Jonason and his colleagues, then at New Mexico State University. Sociopaths are also more likely than most to have more sexual partners and a greater tendency to have casual, short-term relationships. Women may be drawn to such men, because they are exciting to be with,[77] thereby contributing to their later victimization.

Other researchers have also found that individuals with psychopathic traits do especially well in business and leadership positions. For instance, Antoine Bechara, a professor of psychology and neuroscience at the University of Southern California, suggested that "the most successful stockbrokers might plausibly be termed 'functional psychopaths,' because they were better at controlling their emotions or didn't experience them as intensely as others, so they could take more calculated and successful risks.[78]

In 2010 when Robert Hare and his colleagues gave the PCL-R to more than 200 top US business executives, they found that the business executives not only had more psychopathic traits than the general population, but "psychopathy was positively associated with in-house ratings of charisma and presentation style: creativity, good strategic thinking, and excellent communication skills."[79] This is also why many psychopaths may be found in positions of wealth in which those who are very competitive, cut-throat, and coercive thrive very well. Likewise, they can readily be found in the higher reaches of power and status in many organizations. As Kevin Dutton sums it up:

"The psychopath seeks reward at any cost, flouting consequence and elbowing risk aside . . .Money, power, status, and control—each the preserve of the typical company director, and each a

---

[75] Ibid., pp. 75-76.
[76] Ibid., p. 123.
[77] Ibid., pp. 101-102
[78] Ibid., pp. 104
[79] Ibid., pp. 105.

sought-after-commodity in and of itself—together constitute an irre-
sistible draw for the business-oriented psychopath as he or she ven-
tures ever further up the rungs of the corporate ladder."[80]

In fact, Bob Hare and Paul Babiak found that the core psychopathic
traits can sometimes become the star qualities characteristic of an influ-
ential leader. As the following chart they developed shows, there are close
parallels between leadership and psychopathic traits.[81]

Leadership Trait	Psychopathic Trait
Charismatic	Superficial charm
Self-confidence	Grandiosity
Ability to influence	Manipulation
Persuasive	Con artistry
Visionary thinking	Fabrication of intricate stories
Ability to take risks	Impulsivity
Action oriented	Thrill seeking
Ability to make hard decisions	Emotional poverty

Today, social conditions may make it even more conducive for sociopaths to operate. As Dutton observes, the new millennium has seen the
rise of a new wave of corporate criminality that far surpasses anything
before, including investment scams, conflicts of interests, entrepreneurial
schemes, and high levels of embezzlement that are now "utterly unprece-
dented. Both in scope and in fiscal magnitude."[82]

Moreover, as Clive R. Boddy, a former professor at the Nottingham
Business School points out, sociopaths/psychopaths can take advantage of the "relatively chaotic nature of the modern corporation,"
including the rapid change, continual change, and high turnover of
key personnel, which enables them to better move into positions and
up the corporate ladder through their key personal characteristics—an
"extroverted personal charisma and charm."[83] Then, as they ascend to
a high position, they can influence the tone of the whole organization
with their power, though the benefit to themselves and their organization can be at the expense of society as a whole. For example, Boddy

---

[80] Ibid., p. 117.
[81] Ibid., pp. 124-125.
[82] Dutton, p. 133.
[83] Ibid., p. 133.

suggests that psychopaths in high positions in the financial world were to blame for the global financial crisis, because of their "single-minded pursuit of their own self-enrichment and self-aggrandizement to the exclusion of all other considerations," which led to the end of a tradition of "noblesse oblige, equality, fairness, or any real notion of corporate social responsibility."[84]

In turn, this influence has contributed to a shift in the moral climate in modern culture, whereby the behavior of the sociopath/psychopath has become more common. Thus more and more people follow their lead, resulting in even more victims due to the growing acceptance of this behavior by all. In other words, as social institutions break down there is more advantage to an "every man for himself" ethos, and in such conditions, sociopaths/psychopaths thrive.

Certainly, one can point to more and more of this behavior in everyday life—in fact, it is glorified in the modern media, such as in game shows like *Survivor* and *Big Brother*, where the most strategic survive, and in films and TV shows which glorify the amoral but quick-witted and charming lead character. Some examples include *Sherlock Holmes*, where Holmes even calls himself a "high-functioning" sociopath, *House of Cards*, about a wily politician who will do anything to win until he succeeds at becoming President, and *Breaking Bad*, in which a once compassionate chemistry professor is transformed into a drug dealer, willing to lie and use any tricks he can, to keep the enterprise going. Even news stories about foreign and homegrown terrorists may have the inadvertent effect of inspiring more sociopaths to be attracted to this activity because of the feeling of being in control while carrying out these acts, combined with experiencing fame from the sudden attention to their actions. By contrast, the victims seem to be of less interest in the stories of the latest mass killings that splash across the Internet news feeds and are highlighted on the TV news and newspapers.

Then, by glorifying the individual with these sociopathic traits and behaviors, they become even more common, as others adopt these characteristics in various ways. For instance, social media newsfeeds often feature individuals engaging in predatory acts, where they are torturing other people or animals or attempting daredevil stunts. Despite the comments that express outrage or call the perpetrators "crazies," there is still a fascination with these videos. People continue to post and repost them, and readily watch and comment on them.

Moreover, the fluidity and anonymity possible in modern society has made it easier for sociopaths to seek protective cover, even as more and more information can be exposed about people every day through the news and social media. One reason for this greater concealment is that

[84] Dutton, p. 134.

sociopaths can easily move elsewhere, should a current position end or a scheme blow up, because they don't have the same need for close relationships as others do. So moving away can minimize their chances of running into their victim.[85] Then, too, sociopaths can easily change their identity to create a new mask, or a new invented resume to establish a new life, which can make punishing them for any past civil or criminal actions difficult. Once in the new location, their charm can help open doors for them, so they can start searching for victims anew.

In short, the upheavals, turmoil, and changing norms of modern society—which glorify materialism, excitement, individual success, and celebrity—are all playing into the hands of sociopaths who can play down their anti-social traits and use their personable wiles to charm victims and achieve success, particularly in certain fields that value the traits the sociopath possesses.

The Many Varieties of Sociopaths

While sociopaths have the classic pattern of traits and behaviors described by Cleckley's 1941 description in *The Mask of Sanity* and in Hare's later Psychopathy Checklist, (a clinical rating scale), unlike the a self-report tests: the PCL-R, and PCL-SV (Screening Version), sociopaths can differ in the degree to which they have different traits. When trained therapists rate individuals on these scales to diagnose them as sociopaths/psychopaths, they score them on different traits and behaviors. Above a certain score, a person is deemed a sociopath, below that the person may have a tendency towards sociopathic traits and behaviors, but isn't so designated.

They rate the person being evaluated through an in-depth interview, and by reviewing the information in the person's records. For each trait or characteristic, the clinician judges whether each quality applies, using a range of 0 (not applicable) to 2 (clearly applicable) with 1 only partially applicable. After the scores are totaled, 40 is the highest score reflecting a perfect psychopath. Commonly a score of 30 is used to identify a psychopath for clinical purposes, or 25 and over for research purposes. Or if a clinician uses a shorter scoring test—the PCL:SV with 12 items—scores range from 0 to 24, where a score of 18 and over is used to designate a psychopath.[86]

Thus, sociopaths can vary in the degree to which they hide certain behaviors which characterize them, in that those at the upper end of the

---

85 Dutton, p. 218.
86 Babiak and Hare, pp. 27-28.

scale have a much greater dose of the interpersonal, affective, lifestyle and antisocial features that define the sociopath. The degree to which any person exhibits psychopathic behavior depends on their mix of qualities and the particular situation that draws them to express these behaviors.[87]

Yet, while there may be this time-tested way of assessing sociopaths by clinicians, one can make an assessment of whether someone is likely to be a sociopath or not by looking at their traits and behaviors. Though not an official therapeutic diagnosis, this is a rule of thumb approach for assessing the people in your life, so you can know how to better deal with people who act like sociopaths. Given the estimate of 4 percent of the population considered to be sociopaths, with most not having been identified as such by the mental health professionals or criminal justice system, this approach seems like a reasonable way to assess whether someone is a sociopath or acting like one.

However, another complication in identifying sociopaths is that they can change over time, such as exhibiting less sociopathic behavior as they get older, much as criminals tend to become less violent and commit fewer crimes as they age. Their basic character may be unchanged since they still may possess the same traits, such as an ability to manipulate and lie to get what they want. But they express more control over expressing those traits in anti-social ways. Perhaps a taming factor may be that they get involved in relationships with family members or get into high business or government positions, so they have more to lose. Plus they have gained more of what they want through earlier acts to take advantage of their victims, so they don't need to struggle for money and power in the same ruthless way. If successful from their past career as a sociopath, they have more, and so they don't need as much anymore, whereas those who are unsuccessful due to their actions may end up in prison, in the mental health system, or back mooching off mom and dad.

Then, too, sociopaths can differ widely in the way in which they use physical or verbal aggression to manipulate their victims, or in whether they randomly pick out their victims or wait for the right time to target a particular person. But whatever the approach, they typically use lies to support whatever they do. For example, in the assessment phase, sociopaths select victims based on their seeming vulnerability and potential for benefits for themselves, though they differ in their approach. As Paul Babiak and Robert D. Hare describe this in *Snakes in Suits: When Psychopaths Go to Work*:

"Some psychopaths are opportunistic predators who will take advantage of almost anyone they meet, while others are more patient, waiting

[87] Ibid., p. 28.

for the perfect, innocent victim to cross their path. In each case, the psychopath is constantly sizing up the potential usefulness of an individual as a source of money, power, sex, or influence. People who have power, celebrity, or high social status are particularly attractive."[88]

Another difference is in occupations, since certain fields are ideal for individuals with certain traits and behaviors where sociopaths excel. For instance, qualities such as the ability to manipulate and control are an ideal fit for someone who takes a leadership position in a company or organization, such as becoming a top manager or CEO. Though sociopaths are typically rule breakers or rule makers who like excitement and stimulation, they may not fit well in a position where they have to perform routine tasks for most of the day. They may not thrive in a highly regulated environment, in which everyone is monitored to see that they are performing their tasks, since sociopaths like stimulation and may feel hemmed in by a highly rule oriented bureaucracy. But if they can fairly quickly work their way to the top of the hierarchy where they are in charge, they might be willing to wait. Or, they may be drawn to creating and running their own company, since they can then make the rules and control their employees. Then, too, any career where they can use their ability to charm and persuade others, such as sales, financial planning, real estate, and being a seminar leader or speaker, can be a natural fit for them.

By contrast, in certain fields, sociopaths may be less likely, such as in nursing, the health professions, and teaching, where nurturing and helping others are much valued qualities. Still, some types of doctors, such as surgeons and psychiatrists, might be more likely to have sociopathic traits, since they exercise a great deal of power and control in their position.

Distinguishing Between a Sociopath and a Narcissist

Another problem in attempting to identify the sociopath is that it can be hard to distinguish a sociopath from a narcissist, with both having many similar traits. Like the sociopath, the narcissist has a grandiose sense of self-importance, is preoccupied with fantasies of unlimited success, power, and brilliance, and believes that he or she is "special" and unique. Similarly, the narcissist seeks excessive admiration, has a strong sense of entitlement, is exploitative of others to get what he or she wants, lacks empathy, often envies others or believes others are envious of him or her, and regularly shows arrogant, haughty behaviors or attitudes. According

---

[88] Paul Babiak and Robert D. Hare, *Snakes in Suits: When Psychopaths Go to Work*, Harper Collins, 2006, pp. 43-44.

to psychologists, the narcissist has at least five of the above traits. So often many sociopaths are narcissists, too.[89]

The key difference would seem to be the sociopath's ability to deceive, manipulate, and control others without a conscience, reflected in their lack of remorse, guilt, or concern for the devastation their acts can wreak on others.[90] Though sociopaths may express remorse at times, they don't really feel it; it is like they are going through the motions, saying what they think is expected as an acceptable social response. One reason for their lack of remorse or guilt is that they are able to rationalize their behaviors and shrug off personal responsibility for their actions, though such behavior may be considered unethical or shocking to those who have played by the rules.[91] But sociopaths readily find excuses for their behavior, may lie and deny something happened, or, even if they acknowledge doing something, they minimize or deny the consequences of their actions on others.[92]

How Sociopaths Stay Out of Jail and the Mental Health System

One question that often comes up is how do successful sociopaths, who are taking advantage of so many victims, stay out of jail? Or how do they stay out of the mental health system?

While some do have encounters with the criminal justice system, such as Victor who was eventually convicted of scamming investors, most are able to evade any penalty. One way is arrange a deal where they make payments for past misdeeds, or the victims are isolated, so they aren't aware that other victims have been similarly taken in by the sociopath. Another problem is that victims may be too embarrassed to come forward, or they may not realize what has happened to them until the very end and the sociopath can readily move away. Or the police may not be interested in pursuing a case, because it seems more like a personal matter, such as when a sociopath uses a partner's or family member's credit card and claims he or she had permission to use it. Or the complaint may seem more like a civil case, such as when the fraud starts with a contract that leads to broken promises and deception.

Another reason that many sociopaths escape doing time or going to a mental health facility, is because they appear to be performing their occupation reasonably well as lawyers, doctors, psychiatrists, academics, business people, or others, without breaking the law or being caught and convicted. Plus many have the advantage of a high intelligence, family

---

[89] Hare, p. 38.
[90] Ibid., p. 40.
[91] Ibid., p. 42.
[92] Ibid., p. 43.

connections, and social skills that enable them to "construct a facade of normalcy and get what they want with relative impunity."[93]

Sociopaths may also evade contact with the criminal justice, legal, or mental health systems because the scams they pull commonly involve a willing victim, at least in the courtship/honeymoon phase, and the victim may not realize they are being victimized until the unfulfilled promises and lies mount up. And some lies and strategies to defraud or exploit the victim can be quite complex to unravel, making it difficult to make a clear-cut case against the sociopath. Then, too, the sociopath's excuses and explanations may complicate a case, when it is a "he said/she said" situation. So the best you can do is create documents in the form of an email trail or keep a regular journal where you record your experiences.

Some Examples of Sociopaths at Work

Stout provides a few examples which illustrate how some conscienceless sociopaths have been able to operate successfully, using composites created from her clients as a clinical psychologist. For example, the successful businessman she calls Skip outwardly presents the image of a super successful businessman, working for a company that makes blasting, drilling, and loading equipment for metal-ore mines.[94] The son of super-rich parents, at thirty he married the twenty-three-year-old daughter of a billionaire who made a fortune in oil exploration, and views his wife as a sweet, repressed society woman who readily accepted her role as wife and social coordinator. He also expected that she would pretend not to notice that he took no personal responsibility and played around through random sexual encounters.[95]

Continuing his success trajectory, at thirty-six, he became president of the company's international division, and at fifty-one, the company's CEO. Along the way, charges of misconduct surfaced, such as when a secretary sued him for breaking her arm while he tried to force her to sit on his lap. But since the company was considered to be so valuable, he covered up these charges of sexual misconduct with a check to the complainant to shut her up, so the company helped to enable his deceptions and lies. When the Securities and Exchange Commission accused him of fraud, he naturally denied the charge, in a case still pending when Stout wrote her book.[96]

[93]   Hare, p. 113.
[94]   Stout, pp. 40-41.
[95]   Stout, p. 41.
[96]   Ibid., pp. 42-43.

These cover-ups and denials are all part of the sociopath's arsenal of lies, used as necessary to enable the sociopath to participate in other behaviors that contribute to success.

Stout gives another example of a thirty-four-year-old woman sociopath, Doreen, who worked in a hospital as an administrator and therapist. As Stout describes it, Doreen used her charm and mask of caring to play nice to the frumpy secretary-receptionist, with Doreen seeing her as someone who could attest to her niceness, while she sought to simultaneously manipulate and destroy one of her colleagues, Jackie, who she viewed as a threat. She especially resented Jackie, because she was beautiful, very smart, and up for a Mentor of the Year Award at the same time as Doreen.

Doreen found a way to discredit Jackie, while undermining the psychological healing of one of Jackie's patients, Dennis, a paranoid schizophrenic. Though Dennis was not one of Doreen's patients, she saw him twice a week as the administrator of his treatment, which involved seeing how his progress was going, checking his paperwork, and approving his discharge once he was sufficiently better to go home. However, while Jackie told Doreen that Dennis had improved and she planned to see him as an outpatient once he was discharged, Doreen told Dennis the opposite. She told him that Jackie said he was much sicker and would never see him outside the hospital because he was too dangerous.

This betrayal caused Dennis to relapse, and he fell into a stunned silence, unable to move. So Doreen had him transferred by two burly mental health workers to a locked ward unit with greater security. She was fairly sure that Dennis would not tell anyone what she had told him, since Dennis was too paranoid to share his secrets. And even if he told anyone, no one would believe him, since no one believes the patients over the doctors. So she felt great satisfaction in causing Jackie to not only lose her VIP patient, but also blame herself for doing something harmful in his therapy to cause his relapse. Later on, another therapist would handle the patient.[97] So score one for Doreen in using a big lie to advance her strategy of undermining her opponent, caring not a bit about what this all did to Dennis.

Later, when Dennis told Jackie what happened and she believed him, Jackie couldn't convince the unit director that anything Dennis said was true. The director encouraged her to not continue the disagreement with Doreen, since that would be bad for the unit, so Doreen got away with lying once again.

Doreen was finally exposed six years later when an outside consumer advocate on a local TV show investigated, because he believed that Doreen's therapy of his depressed wife was undermining his marriage. After he discovered that Doreen didn't have the claimed credentials, he said he would

[97]   Stout, pp. 70-76.

broadcast this information if the hospital didn't forgive his wife's hospital bill. The hospital's business director fired Doreen and disputed her claims that the consumer advocate was lying because he did not like her.[98] So finally Doreen's lies were exposed, and she was defeated—a result that generally doesn't occur when a single victim is the target of a sociopath's lies. But such a defeat can occur when enough victims come forward to reveal a pattern of lies, or when someone powerful enough comes forward to expose the truth.

This situation is similar to what I experienced myself in two cases. One was a therapist who hired me to write a memoir and lost her license for mistreating her patients. The other time involved a power-hungry creative director at an ad agency I worked for, who sought to destroy the supervisor of my department.

In the first case, I met Melody the therapist writing her memoirs through the National Speakers' Association, where I was promoting my writing services to speakers. She told me she wanted to include a chapter on US history from the Depression to the 1990s, to show what conditions were like while she was growing up and later working as a therapist. The first hint that she had little concern for the truth was when I told her some details and dates were wrong. She wasn't interested in my doing any research to correct this, saying that any research would be too time-consuming and costly. Another red flag was that she made claims for her extensive achievements without any supporting detail. When I tried to ask for more information, such as names and dates, she shut down any further discussion by telling me: "Don't worry about it. You have to understand, I like to control things. I'm in charge." Her statement was a sign that she might be a sociopath, since a sociopath always has to be in control and right, even in the face of evidence of errors, though I didn't know anything about sociopaths at this time.

The kicker came when I overheard some conversations with her attorney, when I was in her office waiting to take notes. The lawyer was representing her in her fight against the California Board of Family Therapists, which was trying to take her license, and she was telling the lawyer that he should claim that the patient was lying to pursue a malpractice claim against her.

Initially, I put what I overheard aside, until Melody decided not to pay me for much of the work I had done. She told me, "I realize I can write this myself, so I don't need you to write it for me."

When I protested that I had already spent many hours writing a first draft, she blew me off, saying, "I'm sorry, but I'm strapped for cash right now."

Though I didn't recognize it at the time, her behavior—blaming her patient for lying in filing a false claim against her and not caring about the time I had spent trying to help—were also signs of the sociopath, being all about self and not having any compassion for others.

[98] Stout, pp. 84-85.

Then, when I investigated her fight with the California Board of Family Therapists, the signs were even clear in the way she mistreated her patients for her own ends and sought to lie to the Board about what she did. In one case, Melody had gotten an obese patient, Deborah, to work for her as an administrative assistant for no pay, claiming that this work would help her feel better about herself and gain experience, since no one would hire her because of her weight. She even charged Deborah, claiming this was part of her therapy. But Deborah was feeling worse about herself as an unpaid employee, and when Deborah's parents learned what was going on, they complained to the Board of Family Therapists.

In the second case, another patient, Lydia, who had problems trusting and had turned away from friends and potential boyfriends, was also working for Melody for free. Worse, Melody borrowed $30,000 from Lydia's parents, claiming she needed this to expand her business and continue helping Lydia's progress from her treatment. But rather than use the money to build her practice, she spent it on clothes and a new car, and she didn't begin repaying Lydia's parents at the time as agreed. So Lydia's parents also complained to the Board of Family Therapists.

Not only were these complaints serious, but Melody claimed these patients were lying, trying to get out of paying for their therapy. But ultimately, the Board didn't believe her excuses and lies, so she lost her license to practice, went through a bankruptcy, and tried to get engagements as a speaker, though that effort didn't go very well.

As in the case with Jeremy, I didn't think of Melody as a sociopath at the time, since she was an apparently successful therapist when I met her, and I didn't know the characteristics of a sociopath. But looking back, all the characteristic traits are there—the external charm, the lack of conscience or concern for others, despite being in a helping profession, and the use of outrageous lies, made more credible as they were spoken by a trusted person in authority.

In the second case, soon after I graduated from college in the late 1960s and got one of my first jobs in an ad agency, I saw firsthand how the agency's Creative Director targeted a popular department supervisor and sought to undermine her through various tactics, including lying. I didn't think to characterize her as a sociopath at the time, since I was just out of school and naive about how the work world worked, and the one course I took in psychology didn't describe any of these characteristics. Psychopaths, as sociopaths were called at this time, were simply evil criminals who terrorized others before being caught and brought to justice, or they were mental cases out of touch with reality who ended up in mental hospitals. There was no indication that sociopaths might be successful in the everyday world, using the same kind of tactics that brought criminals and mental patients to the attention of authorities. However, they used these methods in a carefully controlled way to achieve success and undermine others through covert schemes so they could carry on for a long time undetected.

At the agency, I was initially hired as a Project Director by the Research Department Supervisor, Eileen, an outgoing, cheerful woman in her early thirties. Our job was to conduct surveys on qualitative research project campaigns, and my team of six Project Directors set up and analyzed focus groups. A separate Creative Group handled the creative text and art work for the ads, Account Executives brought in the business, while Media Buyers selected and bought the media placements in radio, TV, newspapers, and magazines. It was the late 1960s, the time glorified by *Mad Men* on TV today, and there was no Internet or social media.

Into this mix stepped Andrea, a pushy woman in her forties, who had that kind of aggressive New Yorker approach to life. She was hired to be the Creative Director in charge of both the Research Department and the Creative Group, and she soon had Eileen in her sights, as someone she wanted to get rid of, while she adopted one of the Research Project Directors, Danny, as her favorite.

Danny was the kind of guy who didn't play by the rules if he could get away with it, such as one time when he removed a half-dozen chairs from the focus group room for a weekend party. While some of the other Research Project Directors might get fired for doing that without permission, being Andrea's pet, Danny could do no wrong. So she simply told him not to do it again or ask for permission, and she would see if she could clear the way for special circumstances.

However, Eileen thought what he was doing was wrong, since the chairs were agency property, and others might want to use their furniture for their own uses. And besides, what if the furniture got damaged when moved? So after Eileen raised this issue at a staff meeting, and Andrea heard about this from Danny, she decided Eileen had to go. It was as if by raising this issue, Eileen had dared to challenge her authority and protégé, so now Andrea was determined to undermine Eileen's position and discredit her to everyone in the agency, so she would be pushed out—much like Doreen sought to undermine Jackie, after viewing her as a threat to her authority, besides having a very attractive appearance and personality.

One of Andrea's strategies was to ask to see copies of the reports from the Research Department, along with any reports and memos which Eileen wrote. Then, she sent them back with critical comments, requiring revisions. So now Eileen had to rework her own material or ask her Project Directors to make revisions, which she then reviewed and sent to Andrea. As a result, Eileen was working much later hours, as were the Project Directors in making revisions. In time, this method slowly worked to undermine their favorable attitude towards her, because they not only had more work, but came to doubt her initial reviews of their reports, In some cases, there were even revisions of revisions.

Secondly, Andrea now cut Eileen out of the distribution list for many memos and reports that she sent out. As a result, Eileen often didn't know about a new policy or directive from Andrea, and when she found out that others were receiving these memos, such as myself and my office mate who were on close terms with her, she began looking to us to find out what she should know. But this effort helped to undermine her authority, since instead of her giving directives, Andrea was giving them directly to the Project Directors, and she had to ask her subordinates what was going on.

Then, upping the pressure even more, Andrea began spreading lies about Eileen, such as when Eileen took four days off to unwind and see a doctor about the growing stress that was causing an ulcer and making her more susceptible to colds and flu. But instead of acknowledging her role in causing Eileen's stress, Andrea told Danny that she thought Eileen was having a nervous breakdown. Danny spread the word, as she knew he would, to the other Project Directors. Thus, when Andrea returned from sick leave, she sensed the growing distance between her and the Project Directors, and their lack of respect and attention to what she said. It was as if Andrea had rendered her into an outsider in the department she once headed, thereby undermining her authority. And, much like Jackie who found no one took her seriously after Doreen targeted her, Eileen felt there was little she could do, since Andrea was the Creative Director with a direct line to the agency's top brass. In fact, making Eileen's situation even more perilous was that Andrea had charmed her way into creating some great advertising campaigns, resulting in increased earnings for the agency.

Convinced there was no way she could win—and probably she couldn't—Eileen resigned from the agency. With her resignation, Andrea had clearly won, and after that her favorite Project Director got the new job.

Looking back, I can now see Andrea's campaign against Eileen as the machinations of a sociopath to get a chosen victim out of the way. She lied and took other deceptive steps to undermine Eileen's authority and ability to do the job, driving Eileen out , since she was a threat, as a young, attractive, popular supervisor. The industries and settings were different, but they used the same basic tactics, whereby a sociopath sets out to destroy a targeted victim, without any concern or feelings of guilt about the damage inflicted, and feels great satisfaction when the mission is finally accomplished.

CHAPTER 4:

THE MANY SOCIOPATHS AMONG US

Who Are the Sociopaths?

Since about 4 percent of the population are considered to be sociopaths by many researchers,[99] that represents about 12.9 million people out of the US population of 322 million. So the potential for encountering and becoming the victim of a sociopath is huge. Thus, this book has been written to help potential victims recognize the traits of a sociopath, so they can avoid being victimized or get out of or reduce the damage from a relationship with a sociopath.

However, one often does not realize one is being victimized at the time, since sociopaths are like chameleons, who can easily assume different identities and play different roles. Their ability to easily transform themselves makes it easy for them to blend in to society without anyone recognizing them for what they are. Another advantage which sociopaths have in manipulating and taking advantage of victims is that most people tend to trust others they regularly work, socialize, or live with. Sociopaths can also seem outwardly adjusted and caring, however they don't have any affection for others and seek to gain what they want at any cost, while they are good at pretending they care. Thus, victims can easily be swayed by a sociopath who outwardly appears to be a compassionate, caring, trustworthy individual, as I and many others have found.

As a result of their ability to deceive, millions of sociopaths live among us, although often they are unrecognized, apart from sociopaths who have come to the attention of mental health and criminal justice professionals, when they exhibit mental problems or get caught in criminal activity. Otherwise, sociopaths can use their intelligence and wiles to readily blend in and sometimes become very successful doing so.

While many sociopaths can easily blend in with those around them, they can be very destructive in harming others who they work with or

---

[99] Martha Stout, *The Sociopath Next Door*, New York: Harmony, 2006.

interact with in their personal life. Some even become criminals, such as Ted Bundy, the notorious rapist and serial killer of at least thirty women in the 1970s. What makes sociopaths especially dangerous is that they can readily do damage in the workplace or in their relationships and then move on without any concern about the harm they have caused. But often those who work or have a personal relationship with a sociopath don't realize they are dealing with one, until they have been taken advantage of or harmed by someone they once trusted, then used that trust against them, as I and many of the people I interviewed experienced.

So you need to be aware of the warning signs, especially if you feel that someone is trying to manipulate or trap you into doing something you don't want to do. By recognizing the common behavior pattern and communication styles, it can help you recognize the sociopath and avoid becoming a victim or reduce the harm in the relationship.

To show how sociopaths find and take advantage of their victims and set the stage for my in depth interviews with about two dozen victims and a few sociopaths willing to talk about themselves, I have discussed the memoirs of two self-identified sociopaths in which they describe how they behaved with others at work and in the personal life. Then, by recognizing how these behavior patterns contribute to victims being victimized by the sociopath, individuals can learn to recognize these patterns when they encounter a sociopath in their own life and act accordingly to avoid becoming victims.

Analyzing How Victims of Sociopaths Become Victims

A basic problem in researching sociopaths is that they lie a lot, though I have assumed that in writing their memoirs, the self-identified sociopaths were honestly describing their experience. I did so, since they wrote their memoirs like confessionals about past behavior and even pointed out that writing often was a way to atone for the harm they had caused. However, since an essential characteristic of the sociopath is telling lies, there is always the possibility that these memoirs are fiction or fictionalized stories anchored in real experiences, perhaps told to conform to the popular image of the sociopath to create a book that sells. So, unfortunately, it can be difficult to know what is true or not, since sometimes sociopaths confuse or intermingle what is real and a lie; or they may write their stories based on their perception of how others perceive and think of sociopaths or how they want to present themselves.

Still, given this caveat, I have sought to understand how the different characteristics and behavior patterns of the sociopath enable them to entrap vulnerable victims. In turn, by better understanding these patterns of behavior, others can avoid becoming victims or reduce the harm done them.

I have done so by examining the experiences of my business associate with the woman producer I previously described and analyzing the already published memoirs of two self-identified sociopaths. *My Name is Amelia, and I'm a Sociopath* by Amy D. Brooks and *Confessions of a Sociopath: A Life Spent Hiding in Plain Sight* by M. E. Thomas, both published in 2013. In doing so, I have looked for common traits and behavior patterns, their effect on the victim, and the victim's response on discovering the lies.

So now let me introduce the victim and sociopaths, and then describe how others can avoid being victimized by looking for the warning signs.

Introducing the Victims

As noted earlier in this book, my own introduction to Sylvia, the film producer, occurred at a film funding conference, when I was just learning about the film industry. And not only did I not notice any of the warning signs because of my lack of knowledge about the film industry, neither did my associate Jerry, who had grown a successful biotech firm involved in manufacturing and selling medical devices to doctors and hospitals. He emigrated to the US from a small country in the Pacific—let's say Indonesia, and has many high level contacts there in government and the business community. I met him because he wanted to get into the film industry to make films fighting social injustice and telling the stories of third world people, and I referred him to several other people in the industry, including Sylvia, since her partner wrote scripts.

That introduction was the beginning of Jerry becoming a victim, too, though I wasn't aware of this for over five years, since Sylvia used her wiles to keep us apart, until after I, too, realized I had been a victim. She kept us apart by claiming that Jerry called her too frequently for advice, so she felt exhausted by his calls and no longer wanted to talk to him. While I thought their communication had ended, during this time, Jerry hired her partner Martin to rewrite his script for $10,000, and he paid Martin $10,000 to be listed as an Associate Producer on a 2007 film Sylvia had previously produced with Martin. He also hired Sylvia and Martin to film a $50,000 documentary for him in Indonesia, though I knew none of this at the time, since Sylvia kept the trip secret from me, and told Jerry not to tell me about the trip or their other arrangements together. She told him not to tell me any of this since I might be upset about her going on this trip rather than working on my film and since Martin didn't want to pay a commission. In turn, Jerry went along with her conspiracy of silence, since, as he later told me, this was "just business" as well as an arrangement between them and me.

Jerry's agreement to go along with their secret arrangement set the stage for his own victimization, since the trip was a disaster. Martin not only didn't follow his instructions about what to film, but he made the film about himself and his travels through the country, rather than about the poor living in third world conditions. Then, after they arrived at the airport in the United States and were about to head for separate planes, to Northern California and to L.A., Sylvia refused to give him the film, claiming that she and Martin wanted to edit the film themselves and give him a completed film, even though he owned the film and hired them to make it.

Though Jerry called them regularly, after six months Sylvia and Martin still didn't give him the film, which is when he called me, accusing Sylvia and Martin of being criminals who had stolen his film and telling me about the trip to the Indonesia. For evidence that he was telling the truth, he sent me some photos from the film shoot, which included meetings with high level members of government. But when I spoke to Sylvia about his call, she not only claimed that she and Martin had a terrible experience due to bad native food and poor accommodations, but she claimed that Jerry was part of a criminal gang that might try to attack her to get back his film. She also urged me to avoid any further contact with him, since this could put her in even more danger, and she falsely claimed that she and Martin were two-thirds partners on the film, so they had a controlling interest and no obligation to give him the film. And they didn't want to give it to him since they feared he would do a cheap edit that would undermine their reputations.

Thus, just as she had done with me six months before, she used a series of lies to keep Jerry from getting back his film, though he had already paid her and her partner and the trip was over. But perhaps it was to play a power game where she enjoyed manipulating and tormenting him, like a cat plays with its prey.

Meanwhile, since Jerry and I didn't talk and compare notes, he continued to be her victim. He was unable to get back his film, despite repeated efforts for five years, and he did not get the Associate Producer credit on the film or in the promotional materials about it. Additionally, he did not get a usable script from Martin, since Martin refused to sign a work-for-hire agreement as promised to assign the completed script to him. And, of course, as a sociopath, Sylvia didn't care. Instead, she seemed to enjoy exercising her control over Jerry while disparaging him to me. Though he went to the police, they weren't interested, claiming it was a civil matter, involving a breach of contract, rather than grand theft, much as my own police department had told me. And when Jerry contacted some lawyers, they weren't interested either, since Sylvia and her partner didn't seem to have any money, and it would be a complicated and expensive suit to pursue.

The Behavior Patterns of the Sociopath's Victims that Lead to their Victimization

As I reflected on the experience that led Jerry, like me, to be ensnared in Sylvia's trap, I noticed several key behavior patterns that contribute to one becoming a sociopath's victim, like an innocent, vulnerable fly drawn to the sociopath's web.

More specifically, the nine major behavior patterns of the victim that contribute to this victimization are these:

- Being an enabler;
- Being naive about the arena in which the sociopath operates;
- Being too trusting, so one is receptive to believing the sociopath's lies;
- Being willing to accept the sociopath's point of view without questioning or seeking additional information to test any claims;
- Not questioning the sociopath's vagueness or contradictions in stories of past achievements or events;
- Being complicit in the sociopath's schemes which might harm others if one will benefit from the arrangement;
- Being receptive to the sociopath's compliments and flattery, while not questioning the blame or criticism of others;
- Being separated from others who might be able to reveal who the sociopath really is;
- Having little recourse on discovering the truth about the sociopath, allowing the sociopath to continue to victimize others.

I'll describe each of these behavior patterns in turn.

Being an enabler.

The victim acts like an enabler, allowing the sociopath to turn him or her into a victim, much like a person in a relationship with an alcoholic, drug addict, or other abuser, who enables the addict to continue the abuse. The classic example described in books, documentaries, and TV specials is the long-suffering spouse, partner, or parent, who puts up with the bad behavior. Such a person repeatedly shows love and concern and tries to help, but those actions only give the addict or abuser more opportunity to continue this destructive behavior. At times, blow-ups or splits in the relationship may occur, after which the addict or abuser promises to reform, so the victim returns or remains in the relationship, hoping things will get better. But commonly things don't improve or they get worse, as the addict takes more drugs and the abuser becomes more abusive. Then, the cycle starts again, often ending when the victim moves out permanently, when the addict or abuser finally gets some effective treatment, or when the addict or abuser goes too far, leading to a deadly overdose or a deadly violent act against the victim.

In turn, the victim commonly remains in an enabling relationship due to continuing to believe the sociopath's explanations and excuses, which are really lies to avoid the victim discovering the sociopath's bad behavior or earlier lies. Then, since the victim wants to trust, believe, or forgive, he or she is willing to return or continue the relationship, thereby enabling the sociopath to victimize them again.

That's what happened to Jerry, when he readily accepted Sylvia's explanations of how things worked in the film industry and how she and her partners could help him. He also did not question her when she asked him not to tell me about his hiring them to film in Indonesia, though I was the one who referred them to him. His willingness to keep silent helped to support Sylvia's scheme to cheat me and later contributed to his own victimization when Sylvia wouldn't return his tapes. He couldn't turn to me for help, because I had believed her claim that he was a part of a criminal gang that might be seeking to kill her and her partner to get the tapes. So Jerry's own actions—or lack of actions—contributed to enable Sylvia to hold onto the film, which her partner later claimed as his own.

Being naive about the arena in which the sociopath operates.

A lack of knowledge about the setting in which one encounters a sociopath also contributes to the sociopath's ability to make claims that are believed, since one does not know enough to contradict what the sociopath is saying.

This situation was particularly true for Jerry, since like me, he was a neophyte in the film business. He was susceptible to claims by a seemingly experienced individual, and he didn't have a community of knowledgeable people he could turn to for advice. As a result, when Sylvia presented herself as an experienced filmmaker with many industry connections, he was impressed by her and had no basis for assessing or testing her knowledge. Also, he wasn't aware of a general tendency in the film industry for people to claim they have high-level positions which they haven't yet achieved, such as being a director or producer, when they didn't have the experience claimed.

Thus, after I referred him to Sylvia and she presented herself and her partner as having extensive film production experience, he was a prime candidate for being taken advantage of again and again. Martin agreed to write his script for $10,000, offered him an Associate Producer credit on their 2007 film for $10,000, and agreed to film his proposed documentary of the exploited poor people of Indonesia for $50,000. However, after Jerry paid, Martin did not provide him with a script he could use by not signing a work-for-hire agreement or assigning script rights to him; Martin never put the Associate Producer credit on the film; and Sylvia refused to give him the footage for the film shot in Indonesia. But Jerry was helpless to do much about these problems at the time, since he didn't know anyone in the industry who could help him.

Being too trusting, so one is receptive to believing the sociopath's lies.

Another quality of the victim that makes them a prime candidate to be victimized is a willingness to trust the sociopath, because he or she speaks with such authority, confidence, and certainty, to seem trustworthy. But as in poker, trust is the sociopath's trump card—the ability to seem believable and compassionate, while looking for and preying upon the victim's vulnerabilities. That is one of the sociopath's key advantages– outwardly appearing to be trusted, while inwardly scheming how to best take advantage of the victim.

In turn, victims who lack experience in industry or in dealing with con artists and sociopaths, are all too ready to trust, as was Jerry when he simply pulled out his checkbook and gave Sylvia a series of checks, with only a brief and vague contract detailing what she and Martin would do for him. But as I discovered as I became more familiar with the film industry culture, industry professionals have a high level of distrust of others, because so many people are not what they seem. Also, people are all too ready to take advantage of others. This is a highly competitive industry with much turnover, as people come with high hopes of success and leave when they don't make it. By contrast, newcomers commonly come from an environment where trust is more likely, such as publishing is for me and health products for Jerry. So in coming from a community of trust, newcomers are more apt to trust and give others the benefit of any doubt when questions of veracity arise.

In fact, since the sociopath's big exaggerations and fabrications fall outside this norm, people aren't normally prepared for such lies, which contributes to them having this propensity to trust and thereby believe the sociopath's lies.

Being willing to accept the sociopath's point of view without questioning or seeking additional information to test any claims.

Related to the propensity to trust is a willingness to accept the sociopath's story, without questioning its accuracy, in part because the victim has limited information or connections for comparing that information with other sources that might be different or contradictory. Moreover, given the tendency to trust, a victim is apt to accept what the sociopath says without trying to verify it, much like one generally accepts the stories of others, unless there is some reason to doubt. But given the sociopath's presentation with confidence and authority, a victim is likely to trust and not doubt.

That's what happened to Jerry, since he didn't seek to test out any of Sylvia's and Martin's claims about their experience in producing a documentary. Also, he had little control when Martin turned the film into more of a promotional piece to present himself as a well-traveled host and interviewer, rather than telling the story of the poor exploited children, which was why Jerry hired Sylvia and Martin to make the film in the first place.

Not questioning the sociopath's vagueness or contradictions in stories of past achievements or events.

While some of the sociopath's made-up stories can be extremely detailed, such as those Sylvia told me about the horrible experiences she and Martin had in Indonesia, other stories about their backgrounds can be extremely vague to conceal the real facts which would present them in a less flattering light. Over time, some of their accounts of events can often be contradictory, but the victim may not notice the discrepancies or think to ask further questions to challenge the sociopath when these contradictions occur.

For example, Sylvia kept Jerry on the string with her stories about how she and Martin were continuing to work on the film, and one time, when Jerry called, she ignored his repeated attempts to get the film back from her. Instead, she tried to reassure him by telling him: "We should get the film edited, since it has such lovely footage," but then she did nothing to edit the film.

Being willing to be complicit in the sociopath's schemes which might harm others if one will benefit from the arrangement.

Another way the sociopath can draw in victims and separate them from others is to make them complicit in their schemes by offering them benefits for participating. Some incentives might be the appeal to greed, power, prestige, revenge, or a desire for justice.

For example, in persuading Jerry to work with her and her partner, she claimed to have access to major players in the film industry and wealthy people who could help distribute his film. At the same time, she used various strategies to keep Jerry from talking to me and me to him. One way is that she appealed to Jerry to become complicit with her in keeping his payments to her and Martin secret from me, on the grounds that he would be working with her and no longer had any obligation to me. And she appealed to me to avoid talking to Jerry, claiming at first that he had become a pest who was bothering her and later because he was an evil man involved with a criminal enterprise out to attack her to get back his film.

Being receptive to the sociopath's compliments and flattery, while not questioning the blame or criticism of others.

Sociopaths can also use positive messages, such as compliments and flattery, to draw in their victims, while using blame or criticism to show off their superiority and make victims feel better about themselves. This approach can help tie the victim to the sociopath, while alienating them from the others who the sociopath disparages. The process is a little like what happens when a teacher or boss heaps flattery on a favored student or employee, while denigrating others, so the favored individual feels better about him or herself and works even harder.

Sylvia did this with Jerry when she first met him by flattering him with praise for his expertise as a businessman, his innovation as a film-maker, and his wonderful contacts with high-level government officials in Indonesia. But later, in talking about Jerry to me, she characterized him as being very dumb and naive; claimed he would make a cheap, unpro-fessional film that would ruin her reputation if she gave it to him; and claimed she had made the contacts in Indonesia herself

Being separated from others who might be able to reveal who the sociopath really is.

One strategy sociopaths sometimes use to keep victims from recog-nizing that they are lying or manipulating them is to keep the victims away from other victims or others knowledgeable about their schemes. They are then unable to compare experiences and expose the contra-dictions in the sociopath's stories. This separation of parties sometimes occurs when a sociopath is leading a double life, or a very public life and a secret one, much like a politician or religious figure outwardly acts as a respectable, solid citizen, but is secretly living a life involved with illegal, criminal, or underground activities or even maintaining another family. Occasionally such dual lives are surfaced by the media to the shock of the individual's family, neighbors, or other commu-nity members. Then, too, a sociopath might tell different stories about events in their life to different victims to manipulate them and keep the victims in different social worlds.

That was one of Sylvia's strategies. She got Jerry to agree not to tell me about his hiring her and her partner Martin to make the film in Indonesia, and at the same time, she got me not to talk to Jerry by painting him as a monster. Then, she reinforced this separation by frequently asking me if Jerry had tried to contact me or if I had spoken to him, with the implication that I shouldn't talk to him out of respect for my relationship with her.

Having little recourse of discovering the truth about the sociopath, allowing the sociopath to continue to victimize others.

Finally, sociopaths target victims who cannot easily expose them or stop them from victimizing others. A victim's isolation or embarrassment is one reason a victim may not be able or willing to do anything. Then, too, the sociopath's actions may be hard to classify as a crime, since any agreements with them make it appear that whatever they have done is more of a civil than a criminal matter. Or they may continue the con for so long that the statute of limitations—usually four years with a written agreement in the civil and criminal justice systems—may have run out.

Another problem for pursuing a case is that a sociopath may have little money– one reason some seek to con a victim. So if there is no money, lawyers have little incentive to take the case on contingency; and it may be too expensive to hire a lawyer to pursue a potentially difficult and expensive case to win, given the wiles of the sociopath. Moreover, criminal justice officials commonly want to see a pattern of victimization among at least several victims to take action. As a result, the sociopath can easily go on to victimize other victims, especially by moving to different jurisdictions.

Jerry experienced that. Although he lost $80,000 from Sylvia's deceptions, he couldn't find a lawyer to take the case on contingency, even if he paid out of pocket costs for court and filing fees, and even if he paid half their fee up front and the other half on contingency, though the costs would be around $10,000 or more. The lawyers' main reasons for refusing a contingency arrangement was that pursuing the case could be a long and difficult process with an unclear outcome, and the statute of limitations might have run out because of the dates of the original agreements, and any claim for a willful copyright infringement claim or defamation claims were uncertain and might be limited. But perhaps the number one reason the lawyers were not interested in taking the case is the defendants might not have any money to collect; and there was little or no publicity value for the lawyer in the case, since no one connected with the case was already a celebrity.

Later, when Jerry contacted the police, FBI, district attorney, and attorney general in his area, as wel as l in L.A. where Sylvia and Martin were based, everyone he spoke with was not encouraging. They told him (much like the police in my area told me) that this sounded like a case for civil litigation, because it had started with a contract. So as of this writing, Jerry has been unable to do anything to get compensation or justice.

CHAPTER 5:

HOW SOCIOPATHS TRAP THEIR VICTIMS

Introducing the Sociopaths

The two sociopaths whose memoirs I reviewed were Amy D. Brooks, author of *My Name is Amelia, and I'm a Sociopath* (2014) and M. E. Thomas, author of *Confessions of a Sociopath: A Life Spent Hiding in Plain Sight* (2013). Since one characteristic of sociopaths is telling lies, one has to be cautious in accepting the truth of their memoirs. But with that caveat, here is an introduction to these two self-identified sociopaths, and their major behavior patterns, which have many parallels with the stories Sylvia told to me and Jerry.

While sociopaths can be found in all walks of life, both Brooks and Thomas describe themselves as professionals or from professional backgrounds, like Sylvia. But, they followed very different paths. Brooks came from a middle income background and experienced a drug-fueled descent to the bottom, while Thomas was a highly intelligent and successful professional with a legal career.

As Brooks describes her life as Amelia, she grew up in a fragile family environment, where her father committed suicide when she was five, and her mother worked to support four children. In 2003, when she was thirteen, her Amelia persona began to appear when she started getting drunk after finding liquor in the laundry room cabinet. Soon she began stealing wine bottles from her mother and brought wine in plastic bottles to school. At fourteen, she began having sex when high, and she enjoyed the physiological fix, and the thrill of doing something taboo. By fifteen, she was arrested for shoplifting, smoked marijuana each day, and was frequently suspended from school for a various of offenses including fighting and truancy, reflecting the sociopath's frequent attraction to impulsive risk-taking behavior.

At sixteen, Brooks decided to live on her own, and took a series of part-time jobs, including working at a fast-food drive-in. Uninterested in going to college or saving money, she quit high school during her senior year, and presented herself as a twenty-year-old college student named

Amelia. She enjoyed drinking and getting high, and began a series of ruses, building one lie on to another, to maintain the desired facade. Though she married a man with a J.D. degree, who helped anchor her and repeatedly forgave her long absences and battles with drugs and alcohol, her drinking and drug-taking led her to experience more and more problems. Repeatedly, she refused to accept that she had an addiction problem, until finally a near-death experience led her to find God. Then, she got into treatment and finally recognized that she was an alcoholic. As a result, she sought to change her sociopathic ways to become a more normal adjusted person, although now single, since her marriage didn't survive her lies and struggles with drugs and drink.

By contrast, Thomas followed a very different path. As she describes, she grew up in a successful, middle class family, where her father worked for a big law firm and afterwards had his own business, although he ran into financial difficulties. Early on, she learned to distrust emotions because of her father's hypocrisy in presenting himself as a giving, generous, good person in his church and community. But behind his outward public appearance, he sometimes behaved badly, such as when he failed to pick up her and her brother when they were young children, because they arrived a few minutes late to the spot where he told them to be. So they had to find their own way home. Thomas even had dreams about killing her father, because she loathed him so much.[100]

As Thomas grew up, she never learned to trust. Instead, she learned to depend on herself and manipulate others to achieve the desired outcome. Rather than appeal to people's love or sense of duty, she appealed to their fear or desire to be loved, and she came to view everyone as objects in a chess game. She also felt no firm sense of self, so her life became a series of reactions to events and impulsive decision-making. Since her own emotional world was stifled, her understanding and concern for an emotional connection with others died away.[101]

Still, Thomas found these uncaring manipulative behaviors gave her a competitive advantage, and she became very concerned with the power structure of the adult world.[102] Early on, too, she frequently sought to manipulate, deceive, and trick adults, and she viewed her childhood acquaintances as moving objects in her games. She lied all the time, stole things, and enjoyed tricking kids into giving her things she wanted. She also found ways to gain power by convincing people that their best interest was in pleasing her. She

---

[100] Thomas, M. E. *Confessions of a Psychopath*. New York: Crown Publishers, 2013, pp. 66-67.
[101] Thomas, pp. 74-75.
[102] Thomas, pp. 76-77.

sought attention from everyone, and lacked inhibition. In short, beginning in childhood, Thomas developed the characteristic traits of the sociopath, which later contributed to her becoming successful in the legal and financial world, while hiding under the veneer of an ordinary caring person.

The Behavior Patterns of Sociopaths that Lead Them to Victimize Victims

As I read the memoirs of the self-identified sociopaths and thought about the victims' experiences that led them to be ideal targets, I noticed a number of behavior patterns of the sociopaths, which helped them victimize others once they identified a prospective victim. They become like predators going after their prey and devouring it once caught. In the extreme, the sociopath can become the serial killer who murders a captured victim, unless the victim can escape. But the everyday sociopaths can exploit their prey at work or in a personal relationship, while maintaining an external facade to blend in with everyone else and gain what they want. Later, once sociopaths becomes very successful, since they feel no empathy for others, they may have no more use for a victim and cast him or her out. It's like they use their victims as stepping stones to attain their goal, and once there, they no longer need to use these steps anymore.

The major behavior patterns I noticed are these:

- Developing the traits of a sociopath in childhood;
- Enjoying the feeling of power from manipulating others;
- Being open to taking risks and seeking thrills and excitement;
- Being very selfish and having a lack of concern for others;
- Being very egocentric, including seeking attention and admiration from others;
- Creating a fictional self to present a better, more successful self-image, while not knowing the real self and leading a double life;
- Telling tall tales and exaggerating to create a more powerful, important, or interesting self, and covering up previous lies with more lies.

I'll discuss each of these in turn.

Developing the traits of a sociopath in childhood

For both women, the traits of the sociopath began early in their childhood or teenage years, triggered by family problems or events in their lives. The common response to handling difficult conditions was turning off their feelings for others and developing the risk-taking win-at-all-costs attitude of the sociopath.

For example, Brooks reports that from early childhood, she felt different from others, and lived a lonely existence, distant from her sisters and other family members—a difference made worse by the death of her father, who committed suicide at forty-nine. In response, she began getting books out of the library on guns and she became very curious about death, feeling that "the confusion and anger" triggered by his death shaped the person she would become. She sought to tune out any emotions and made up a fictional story in which she told a counselor that she had a brother who recently died and the family buried him in the backyard.

Brooks also began a pattern of lying early. She frequently faked illnesses to avoid school, and by age ten, Brooks reports she was "infamous around school and our neighborhood for my tall tales."[103] She often used her sisters as victims to show her power and control, such as by taking and hiding their things and promising to return them when she got what she wanted from them. And she loved the feeling of the power over them. As she put it: "I hated being helpless and needed to feel in control over something."[104]

By sixth grade she was smoking marijuana and taking pills, and she began drinking by seventh grade.[105] By thirteen, she was meeting older men online. When her mother found her intoxicated and found loot she had shoplifted, as well as marijuana, and several wine bottles hidden in her toy chests, she punished Brooks by sending her to summer school. But Brooks rebelled there, too. For example, to get out of taking notes, she claimed she had broken her arm and got another student to photocopy them for her. But she never read the notes and skipped most of her classes to drink and smoke weed, though she did well in school by being a good listener.[106]

Thus, early on, for Brooks, the stage was set for a pattern of sociopathic behavior that continued into her teen and adult years.

Similarly, M. E. Thomas describes a pattern of sociopathic behavior dating back to childhood. For example, she had several experiences that led her to distrust others and to feel she had to trust in herself, such as when her mother failed to pick her and her brother up after school at a city park. In turn, this lack of trust in others led her to feel no empathy for them. Instead, early on, she felt distant from others and learned to view them as pieces in a chess game, since she loved to manipulate and exercise power over others. Moreover, she developed no definite sense of self, so she felt driven to react to contingencies and made decisions

[103] Brooks, p. 3.
[104] Brooks, pp. 179-180.
[105] Brooks, p. 3.
[106] Brooks, pp. 31-33

without any guiding purpose. She came to feel indifferent toward feeling love, because her own emotional world was stifled, and she lost the ability to understand and respect the emotional needs of others.[107]

Like Brooks, Thomas also became fascinated with the power structure of the adult world and how the world worked, so she could manipulate others, including other adults. Instead of forming real connections with her childhood acquaintances, she saw them as objects she could move around in her own games. To get what she wanted, she frequently lied and often tricked children into giving her things, and she stole things, too. At the same time, she was often charming and able to delight others in her desire for attention, while at other times, she would withdraw into herself, as if no one was around and she had become invisible.[108]

When she was sixteen, her mother sent her to a therapist to get some emotional help. But for Thomas, this meeting came too late, since she had no intention of changing. She had already come to see the world as a series of opportunities to win or lose in a "zero-sum game," and she used every encounter with others to gain information she could use to her advantage. What she found most useful about therapy was learning what was expected of her to be a normal person, so she could better disguise herself to appear normal and more effectively manipulate others.[109]

Enjoying the feeling of power from manipulating others

Enjoying power and manipulating of others are traits that begin early and are characteristic of the sociopath throughout life. In turn, creating an elaborate facade of lies can support this use of power and manipulation.

For example, Brooks describes how she created a "Jewish Fable" to reframe herself as a "fake Jew" in order to marry a Jewish man, since as a child, she frequently heard her mother say that "Jewish men make the best husbands." As a result, at fifteen she began to adopt various Jewish practices, such as eating kosher and celebrating the Sabbath every Friday night. Then, she began to imagine the ideal husband. To find him, she joined Jewish dating sites, began corresponding with a twenty-year-old economics major, and maintained contact over the years through emails, phone calls, and meetings in various cities. For a time, she created a fictional boyfriend, who had a checkered and exciting past, which included running an underground prostitution ring and belonging to the Russian mafia. Eventually, she claimed he was framed by the NYPD for drug possession and went to prison, so she no longer needed him in her life and moved in

---

[107] Thomas, pp. 74-76.

[108] Thomas, p. 79.

[109] Thomas, pp. 95-96.

with her real boyfriend, though she crafted another story to show she was his educational equal. She claimed she had graduated from NYU with a bachelor's degree in 2008, and to maintain the ruse, she subscribed to the NYU alumni newsletter, toured the campus, and even used her "BA" to land a job as a management trainee at a department store, since the hiring manager had also graduated from NYU.[110]

Finally, after persuading her man to marry her soon after their engagement, Brooks invented a story to get a valid state-issued ID, since she couldn't use the fake IDs she had used over the years. So she came up with an "Adoption Fable" that she had been adopted from a Soviet Union orphanage, and Amy had been her name there. To maintain this charade, she cut off connections with her real family,[111] and to maintain her college-educated fictional narrative, she began an extensive program of reading when home for work and watched news programs, so she could readily discuss the humanities, sciences, and current events.[112] But after successfully maintaining the fiction for about a year, hoping to start over with this new identity, gradually her sense of sadness, anxiety, rage, and feeling trapped into this new identity led her to seek consolation in drinking. This in turn led her to increasingly show another major trait of the sociopath—taking risks and seeking excitement.

This pattern of seeking to gain power over, manipulate, and lie to maintain the fiction was a key part of Thomas' experiences, too, and she found these traits well-suited to achieving success as an attorney and law professor. She viewed morality as serving an instrumental purpose, and when practical and desirable, she followed conventional rules. But otherwise, she chose her own course and felt little need to justify her actions. So she acted without guilt or moral responsibility and with only self-interest in deciding what to do, making her choices through a cost-benefit analysis, rather than due to moral values.[113]

Later, manipulation continued to be her modus operandi as she moved from college to the workplace and eventually into higher status positions of power. One key to this success was her ability to pretend to conform to societal expectations. Yet, while she was a master manipulator, underneath that mask, she wasn't sure who she really was, since she had no clear self-identity apart from manipulating and controlling others and appearing in various guises, like an actor in a stage play.[114]

Then, in law school, she found a perfect fit for her desire to manipulate others and win at all costs, since the students were encouraged to view

[110] Brooks, pp. 13-14.
[111] Brooks, pp. 15-16.
[112] Brooks, pp. 15-19.
[113] Thomas, p. 16.
[114] Thomas, p. 152.

their successes in a zero-sum game measured by precise numbers. After she graduated and got a job at a top L.A. law firm, she delighted in the power games in her office and used her knowledge of others' insecurities to manipulate both junior and senior partners. Like a poker player, she looked for the unconscious tells or small changes in behavior or demeanor that let her know whether someone had a strength or weakness in something. In one case, she got a senior associate to tell her some revealing personal information, about her job insecurities and her attraction to women, after which the senior associate felt intensely embarrassed, and Thomas used the associate's fear of being revealed to others in the firm to gain a three-week paid vacation.[115]

Later, when Thomas became a prosecutor in the DA's office for a short time and worked on misdemeanor cases, she found the job a perfect fit with her traits as a sociopath, because, as she put it: "I'm cool under pressure. I charm and manipulate. I feel no guilt or compunction."[116]

Subsequently, when Thomas worked in the public defender's office, she found being a sociopathic lawyer ideally suited for this role, because she didn't have to judge her clients' moral failings; she just stuck to the letter of the law and ruthlessly tried to win by working every angle. And she liked to win as much for herself as for her clients.[117] She also found the courtroom trial a perfect arena for a sociopath to express this drive to power and manipulate others.

In turn, this drive for power and love of manipulation are traits that can provide a path to success for sociopaths who don't slip into mental illness or get arrested for criminal activities, since these traits help one excel in certain fields, such as being an investment banker, military officer, politician, or business leader. In turn, the association of these traits with being a sociopath can lead one to wonder about the achievements of many present day leaders and great leaders throughout history. Perhaps underneath the outer charm and panache of many high profile celebrities and public figures and their impetus to seek power and manipulate others to gain success, there is a sociopath hiding in plain sight.

Being open to taking risks and seeking thrills and excitement

The willingness to take risks and seek thrills and excitement is another defining trait of a sociopath, and both Amy Brooks and M. E. Thomas describe how this trait influenced their lives. Sociopaths don't like routine,

---

[115] Thomas, pp. 161-162, 165-166.

[116] Thomas, p. 170.

[117] Thomas, p. 171.

and since they don't experience the usual emotions, they can be fearless and take chances.

For example, after Brooks spent a year trying to have a normal life as Amelia, she consciously decided to "go all out" not only with her drinking but with her "deceptions, thieving, and drug use." She did so after concluding that this was who she was, and there was no use pretending she could "*ever* lead a *normal* life." As a result, she began visiting bars after her shift at the mall, and within a few weeks, she began drinking in clubs in L.A. and even Tijuana. She explained these long nights away from home by lying to her husband, telling him she was working graveyard shifts. Frequently, she met random strangers at bars and ended up in their homes for "impromptu after parties."[118]

After losing her job, due to frequent absences and using customer charge account information to open accounts in their name and use their money, she spent every day watching TV, drinking, and smoking marijuana. At the same time, she spent more time online as Amelia playing out her fantasy double life, and she enjoyed pulling strangers into her fantasies.

Amelia thus became a more successful alternate self, whereby she turned herself from an uneducated, unsuccessful woman with a drinking problem into a "cultured, talented, and acclaimed woman."[119] It was her way to pretend to be everything she wanted to be.

Additionally, Brooks creating an alias led to a more exciting fantasy life. In her case, she carried on a variety of extra-marital pursuits with men she met at bars, at parties, and online. She especially liked meeting married men, because they provided "the kind of secretive, risqué encounters that I craved." Though she wanted to come home to her attractive, intelligent, and successful husband, she still wanted to live as if she were single. As part of her risk-taking, she even began taking trips to Mexico to buy drugs and bring them back over the border by packing the pills in small bags hidden in her bra. As a "well-dressed and spoken white woman," she eluded discovery, although she was taking a big risk of getting caught.[120]

After a time, her addiction increased to using all kinds of drugs along with her heavy drinking, and she used various schemes to obtain these narcotics, such as going to different emergency rooms around the area to report phony muscle injuries, as well as buying pills in Mexico. She also supported her risky drug-fueled lifestyle by lying to her husband, claiming she was taking the drugs for a seizure disorder, so passingout each night and forgetting what had happened was a side effect of these pills.[121]

[118] Brooks, pp. 21-22.
[119] Brooks, p. 24.
[120] Brooks, pp. 28, 58.
[121] Brooks, pp. 86, 88.

While Brooks's search for excitement, risk-taking, and lies led to a dangerous downward addiction spiral, Thomas was similarly willing and eager to take risks. But in her case, taking risks contributed to her success as a lawyer, such as when she raced the clock to meet deadlines rather than feeling stressed. This propensity to take risks led Thomas to be very successful in the stock market, too, since this enabled her to think opposite the pack. The drive for excitement also contributed to her success as a law professor, since she became skilled at standing out both in teaching and in making presentations at academic conferences. She simply loved saying outrageous things and having people challenge her, because she liked the controversy. As she put it: "I want people to hesitate before challenging me again. I want them to be afraid to call my bluff."[122]

Paradoxically, though raised as a Mormon, Thomas was drawn to the excitement of seduction, such as when she went to Brazil at eighteen as an exchange student and enjoyed using manipulation to make her conquests fall in love with her. Later, as an adult, she continued to treat love as the ultimate game of seduction, through which she sought mastery and power. She treated it much like sport fishing, or as she described it:

> "The fun is in catching the fish, not in gutting, cleaning, and cooking the fish afterward, so why not throw the fish back to be caught another day? I try to cultivate a persona that makes seduction easy . . .The pleasure of a seduction conquest lies in both the physical satisfaction and the mental challenge of completely occupying a space in a person's mind until it's yours, like a squatter."[123]

Then, too, for the sociopath the excitement of the chase and conquest is mixed with the pleasure that comes from making one feel desirable; it helps to increase the sociopath's self-love. On the one hand, she felt a sense of ownership and gratitude in her relations with family and friends, but with others, she enjoyed exploitation, because, as she put it "The pleasure is in gaining and exercising influence over them . . .I pursue them because they give me a thrill. . . . It is a game, but I am not necessarily interested in the spoils so much as the maneuvering."[124]

Other characteristics and behavior patterns

The other characteristics and behavior patterns of the sociopaths include these, which are closely related to the traits already described. These key traits and patterns are the following:

[122] Thomas, pp. 83, 194-195.
[123] Thomas, p. 236.
[124] Thomas, pp. 246-347.

Being very selfish, including having a lack of care or concern for others

Both Brooks and Thomas frequently did whatever they wanted for their own benefit, without regard for the effect of their actions on others.

For example, Brooks engaged in frequent deceptions to continue to engage in extramarital relationships with other men and to take drugs, and she lied to her husband about her background to entice him into marrying her. Then, she used him to fulfill her own desires, such as using his credit references to get another car, for which she had no intention of paying after the initial month.

Thomas similarly often sought her own benefit while harming others, such as manipulating many junior and senior lawyers she worked with in a large law firm.

Being very egocentric, including seeking attention and admiration from others

Being egocentric is closely related to being very selfish and having little concern for others, and both Brooks and Thomas liked taking center stage and gaining adulation from others, much like an actor glories in raves from the audience. To a great extent both gave a fictive performance by creating an external veneer as they presented themselves to others. While Brooks put on an alternate persona to seem like an educated, successful person, Thomas used this fictional persona to show that she cared and was concerned about others to gain social acceptance.

Creating a fictional self to present a better, more successful self-image; not knowing the real self; and sometimes leading a double life

Creating a fictional self is a way to appear different or better than one is, and sometimes, this fictional self can be so elaborate that it turns into a double life. For Brooks, the desire to seem more successful and educated turned into using multiple aliases and fictional stories to support these different identities. She used so many aliases and stories that she lost track of what was really true about her by the time she was twenty-two. Soon she was leading a double life, where she appeared to be a respectable married woman, but was using false identities to score drugs, pass through customs in Mexico, and carry on liaisons with multiple men."[125]

By contrast, Thomas created a fictive self to conceal her manipulative behavior, and make it seem she cared when she really didn't. For instance, in college, she came to recognize that she lacked a real self under her outer

---

[125] Brooks, p. 76.

layer, after she developed a close friendship with a classmate and got caught looking through the girl's personal letters and journals. After that, the other girls in college shunned her, and during this period of social isolation, she looked closely at herself and realized her lack of self, noting that:

> "I had come to believe certain things about myself that weren't really true. . . . All of the stories I had recently been spinning about my life were illusions. . . . Without actively spinning stories, I had no self."[126]

Since Thomas felt she had no core self, this meant she was free to put on different guises, such as seeming to be caring in personal relationships. To experience love and belonging, she learned to mimic emotional connections and found she could shut herself on or off or open herself up to emotions from fear to anger to joy by flipping an internal switch.[127]

Sometimes, though, she found it difficult to show the appropriate emotional display, such as when she told friends her father had a heart attack. Though she tried to act sad and devastated, she found it hard to accurately fake a sadness which she did not feel.[128]

Telling tall tales and exaggerating in order to create a more powerful, important, or interesting self, and covering up previous lies

Finally, the sociopaths use exaggerated lies in order to create a false persona to manipulate others in their quest for personal aggrandizement and power. Brooks was especially creative in doing this by creating a series of false identities to achieve her goals, including inventing a fake Jewish persona to attract and marry the man she wanted. She created other false personalities to pursue her drug addiction and extramarital affairs. Likewise, Thomas frequently lied, such as in spinning stories for juries while working as a practicing lawyer, and when she invented a persona for the evening so she would feel comfortable attending the cocktail parties she hated.[129] Should any stories be questioned, Brooke and Thomas told still more lies.

---

[126] Thomas, pp. 151-152.
[127] Thomas, p. 204.
[128] Thomas, pp. 207-208.
[129] Thomas, p. 296.

CHAPTER 6:
THE RELATIONSHIP OF VICTIMS AND SOCIOPATHS

The Predator-Prey Relationship

Given the characteristics of sociopaths, particularly their desire to seek power, manipulate, and use people to gain what they want, it is easy to see how they might ensnare their victims. They look for the vulnerabilities of prospects, and find individuals especially prone to becoming victims who are not knowledgeable, willing to trust, and see them as an authority. In turn, the sociopath's confidence helps to assure prospective victims he or she has the necessary knowledge and connections to help the victims gain what they want, so a prospect more likely to fall into the sociopath's trap.

Thus, there is a kind of spider-fly, predator-prey relationship between sociopaths and their victims. Once a victim falls into their trap, it can be hard to escape, since the sociopath's ability to lie convincingly and repeatedly are like lures leading the victim deeper into the trap. This is why, for example, one sometimes reads stories of wealthy older men and women looking for love, who are convinced by a sociopath to give them more and more money, until the victim, fleeced of their money, is of no further use, and the sociopath is on to the next. In some cases, the victim even turns up dead!

This predator-prey relationship occurs because this is an enabling or co-dependent relationship between sociopaths and their victims, whereby the responses of trusting, willing victims enable the sociopaths to achieve their quest for power and manipulation, getting the victims to do what they want. And if one victim escapes their clutches, there are always many more victims to snare, just as a victim who escapes might later be drawn into the clutches of still another sociopath. However, a knowledgeable, potential victim might elude the trap by being aware of the characteristics and behavioral patterns of the sociopath, so they know to stay away.

How to Avoid Becoming a Victim

Based on the traits and behavior patterns previously described, the following recommendations can help individuals avoid being victimized by a sociopath, or end or reduce the damage from the relationship. These guidelines can also help you avoid becoming a victim in a business or personal relationship with anyone generally, such as by exercising caution, gaining knowledge, and not being too ready to trust without sufficient information.

Here are the key warning signs; then you can decide what to do.

- If a person continually gives you excuses and explanations for why things are going wrong without sufficient evidence to support these claims, these excuses and explanations could be the lies of a sociopath trying to avoid blame or responsibility. Once you become suspicious, ask questions of the person to get more supporting information. If the person seems reluctant to tell you more, test out your doubts about his or her sincerity.
- Learn about a new industry or arena in which you are working, so you become more knowledgeable; then a sociopath will be less able to use your naiveté and lack of knowledge to take advantage of you. If the person is telling you how things are in an industry or area that's new to you and that person has something to gain from a relationship with you, such as getting your money, this person could be a sociopath rather than a mentor who just wants to be helpful. So, check out your suspicions. Look for others in this new environment to talk to about how things work, and see if they confirm what your acquaintance, associate, or prospective business partner has been telling you. If not, stay away.
- Don't be overly trusting when you meet new people, since your willingness to trust is a weapon that a sociopath can use against you. Accordingly, don't rush into a relationship where an individual is seeking something valuable from you, such as money or a commitment to a business or personal relationship. Be especially cautious if the other person asks for a quick decision. Don't only consider your immediate intuitive or gut reaction, which could be wrong. Instead, use your emotional response as one indicator and look for more information to support your initial feelings.
- Be willing to question or seek additional information to test out the individual's claims or point of view, especially if you find traits that are common to sociopaths, such as if the individual has a pattern of criticizing and disparaging others, evading responsibility, or showing a lack of empathy and understanding of others.
- Ask questions if you find that someone in a work or personal relationship is commonly vague or tells contradictory stories, especially as your

relationship becomes closer. These are patterns which sociopaths exhibit due to not remembering what they said when they lied to one person or due to them getting confused because they told different lies to different people.

- Avoid participating in or becoming complicit with a scheme that hides important information from someone who should commonly be told this information or if concealing the information might harm someone else. Such a scheme could be especially troubling since later this person might later pitch someone else on a scheme that harms you.

- Be wary if a person frequently compliments and flatters you, while blaming or criticizing others. Such compliments and flattery could make you feel good and more receptive to going along with the individual's designs, while the blame and criticism applied to other people can contribute to your being wrongly distanced from others who have been unfairly cast in a bad light. So pay attention if you think the flattery seems over the top, and look for supporting evidence to show that any criticism or blame of someone else is justified. If not, this could be a sociopath trying to put down others to separate you from them.

- Be cautious if you feel a person is trying to keep you from talking to others, when you might otherwise want to or need to talk to them This separation could be a strategy to conceal contradictory stories or secrets. Certainly there are times when you are justifiably asked not to contact or communicate with another person, such as when someone is representing you or negotiating a deal for the group. But if a call for secrecy seems excessive or unwarranted, be cautious, since the person could be inappropriately manipulating you.

- If you feel that you have been a victim of a scheme, be ready to come forward or inform others about what happened. This information can help you gain recompense or justice in your case, and can let others know about the situation so they can avoid becoming victims, too. However, when taking any action, be cautious so you don't put yourself in a compromising or dangerous position; otherwise, be willing to share your experience reactively or proactively, since secrecy and a lack of communication by victims helps to perpetrate these schemes.

- Pay attention when you are around someone who enjoys having power over and manipulating others, if you start to feel that the person is unfairly or inappropriately seeking to manipulate and control you. Also notice if the exercise of power seems excessive, such as when a boss seems to be playing power games in putting down employers in front of a worker or in turning employees against each other. Should you feel you are being manipulated to do uncomfortable things, that's when to notice more and be cautious about what is happening. If any of these things happen, as appropriate, strategically resist the manipulation, discuss the issue with the person you feel is manipulating you, distance yourself from the manipulative person, or withdraw from the relationship entirely.

- Be cautious if you find someone is very self-centered and seems to show a lack of care or concern for others, or has a pattern of alienating others. While it is common and expected for people to act out of self-interest, they should also show care and concern for others and want to have good harmonious relationships, or maybe you don't want to associate with them. Thus, be cautious when someone seems overly self-involved and frequently engages in actions that put down or harm others or create hostilities with others.

- Be cautious when someone seems too eager to take risks and seek thrills and excitement. Someone with this outlook can have great success when risks pay off, and he or she can bring much fun and enjoyment to your life. But sometimes this behavior can lead to great losses or to a spiral of self-destructive behavior, when the risks don't pay off or the thrills and excitement have negative consequences. Another reason for caution is that, given a sociopath's love of power and manipulating others, you could be led into a situation where the risks could lead to danger.

- Another time to be cautious is if someone is very egocentric and frequently seeks attention from others. While seeking some attention and admiration is normal, if it's excessive, it's often a sign the person is very self-centered and shows a lack of concern for others. This behavior might also be linked to the pattern of putting down and alienating others to aggrandize oneself.

- Be cautious, too, when you see indications that a person has created a fictional self, usually to create a more successful self-image or to lead a double life. Sometimes a person will put on a fictive self to create a better self-presentation in public such as the normally quiet, shy person who becomes ebullient and outgoing in public. But sometimes living a fictive life is a way to hide a secretive, dark side—or perhaps their real life, and the people in each life don't know about the other. Should you notice a split in a person's personality or have intimations of a double life, this is a good time to assess your relationship with this person, and decide whether to continue the relationship, gradually distance yourself, or pull out immediately.

- Another time for exercising caution is when a person continually tells tall tales and exaggerates, usually to appear more successful or interesting, or if you suspect a person is using one lie to conceal another. While it can sometimes be tempting to dismiss the tale telling and exaggeration as a charming quirk, be careful, because you may not be able to discern what is true or not. Then, too, you can get caught up in a series of lies told in a convincing way. As one lies builds on another, you are led to act on these lies in a way that is harmful to yourself or to others.

Sometimes a good strategy is to bring the suspected lies into the open or end the relationship and walk away.

In sum, this advice to be cautious when you observe certain patterns of behaviors can be useful in relationships generally, and individually, anyone can engage in these behaviors. But as you see someone engaging in more and more of these behaviors, it could be an indication this person could be a sociopath, and you need to take care that you are not hurt by the person's actions when they are directed against you.

PART II:

THE MANY FACES OF THE SOCIOPATH

The following section represents the results of my interviews with victims and sociopaths, about the behavior of sociopaths in different settings. These chapters deal with: 1) living with a sociopath, 2) having a work and personal relationship with a sociopath, and 3) having a strictly business relationship with a sociopath.

Behavior and Lies

Is the person who behaves like a sociopath really a sociopath? Classically, a sociopath needs the condition diagnosed by a psychiatrist or other mental health practitioner. However, few sociopaths are actually diagnosed this way. Thus, one is left with the characterized behavior patterns and traits and the way others define someone with whom they have had a business or personal relationship or someone who they have just read about or observed in action on news videos. This behavioral approach is the one I have used in selecting people to interview or in citing the stories I have read about or viewed online.

The use of lies creates a protective shield or weapon for attack which sociopaths use, much more often than the average person. I began thinking of the way lies can be used to defend or attack in a variety of situations, ranging from activities in public, at work, and in one's personal life. These are like zones around the individual which go from the more personal to society as a whole.

An example of these zones of action looks something like this, originally published in my book *Making Ethical Choices, Resolving Ethical Dilemmas*, now published by Changemakers Publishing.

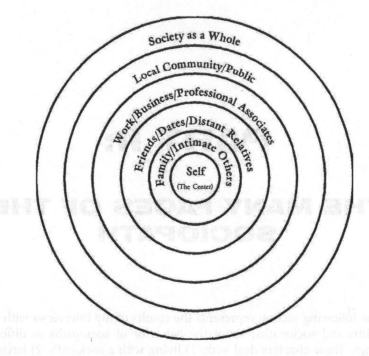

The nature of the lies may differ, since they are created for different situations in different zones of life. But the overall pattern of behavior is the same.

Certainly, one cannot always be correct in inferring that someone is a sociopath by observing or interacting with them in a very small number of encounters. But one might make a good guess timate of a person's thoughts, beliefs, feelings or lack of feelings, and intent based on the circumstances. The process is much like what a prosecutor seeks to do in showing if someone has a *mens rea*, or general or specific intent sufficient to indicate they intended to commit a certain crime, which is defined by having the necessary *mens rea* to commit it. In the criminal justice system, having a *mens rea* needs to be brought out by evidence that certain actions or lack of actions reflect a person's interior thoughts, beliefs, feelings, and attitudes that contribute to this required criminal intent. But people every day draw on their own perceptions beliefs of how and why people act as they do to help facilitate and social relationships, for one has to continually make guesses about people's meanings based on what they say or how they act. In everyday communication, these guesses become second nature; we don't think about them and we learn to behave in a way we consider appropriate in response to whatever else the person says or does. By the same token, we may come to judge someone else as behaving normally or like a sociopath, though the sociopath's skill in wearing a mask can conceal this identity from others.

Behaving Like a Sociopath and the Views of Others

I began thinking about how sociopaths can use lies to support their behaviors in different settings when an associate heading a school told me about a student who sought revenge on another student, and also when I followed the Oscar Pistorius trial online. These were very different settings and stories—but the classic pattern of behaviors commonly engaged in by sociopaths were there in both cases.

In the "less famous" case, a student in a small professional college, let's call her Jean, harbored a long-term resentment against three other students, Meg, Betty, and Veronica, though outwardly, Jean acted friendly and helpful to the others. Then came the time to take the final test, which was half of the students' grades, based on entering the answers on a multiple choice answer sheet.

After the test, Meg, Betty, and Veronica thought they did very well, and were surprised when the instructor called them in to tell them they had failed, so they didn't graduate, because their overall marks weren't high enough. The instructor was surprised, because the three had been good students, but he felt he couldn't pass them because of such low grades.

That would have been that, had one student not come forward with the truth. She told the instructor that she had heard another student say that Jean had been bragging about how she was able to go into the instructor's office, pick up the test answer sheets, and change the three ladies' answers, so they would be wrong on many questions, and return the answer sheets with the wrong answers. The instructor was flabbergasted, but soon remembered how he had often left the office unlocked for a few minutes, during the times he would go to the rest room or get a snack. After he asked around to see if anyone saw anything unusual, another student said she had observed someone going into and out of his office, but didn't think much about it at the time. Eventually, the instructor traced back the chain of students to discover two friends of Jean's who heard her bragging about changing the exam.

At first Jean tried to lie her way out of everything. She talked about only going into the instructor's office to look for him. She acted surprised that anyone could think she would change exam answers. But the instructor confronted her with the results of his own investigation, which led him to discover a hallway videocam, which showed her proudly proclaiming how easy it was to sneak out the answer sheets to make changes and sneak the test back in again. So clearly Jean was caught and had to confess. Ultimately, she was the one who was suspended, and the instructor invited Meg, Betty, and Veronica to retake the exam, which they all passed, so they could graduate.

Why had Jean done what she did, while outwardly acting like a friend to the three women? As it turned out, she was jealous of their success in school. She imagined if they flunked out, she could be one of the top three students. She felt great pride at seeing them flunk and imagining herself receiving honors on stage during the graduation. So she initially lied to appear that she had no reason to harm the three women, and she lied again to get out of being blamed for their failure, until it became too late to make any more excuses—her real intentions toward her victims were on tape.

Though at the time Jean was never considered a sociopath, her "destroy the enemy" approach to cause the three women to fail the exam and flunk out of school was just how a sociopath would behave—doing whatever is necessary to remove any obstacles to her goal of being in the top three in her class, since she thought that would help her find a job in the field after graduating. She didn't care about the damage it might do to the three students, so she lied until she was caught and had no way to explain away her lies.

Right around the time I heard her story, I was also following the Oscar Pistorius trial and saw the parallels. In his well-known story, he claims he heard an intruder, got out of bed without checking if his girlfriend was beside him in bed, blasted four shots into the locked bathroom door, killing his girlfriend, and then yelled, sobbed, tried to revive her, and called to get help. Conversely, the prosecutors argued that Pistorius had an argument with his girlfriend, and after she fled into the bathroom to escape his anger, he shot her, and later sought to cover up his actions by claiming it was all a terrible accident.

Was it? Or was Oscar using lies to cover up what happened by claiming he thought he was shooting at an intruder, instead of feeling real guilt for what he had done. In rendering the verdict, the judge concluded that the prosecution couldn't prove he had the necessary intent—the *mens rea*—to prove murder, although she found him guilty of culpable homicide for negligently firing the gun into the bathroom door. Yet, without a confession of what he was actually thinking and feeling, how could the prosecutor prove his intent? So for five months, the trial went on, as Pistorius and his defense lawyers sought to convince the jury of his side of the case, while some evidence even suggested that he was taking acting lessons to help him show the proper behavior and emotions to portray his deep grief and guilt for what he had done.

Yet, while Pistorius's strategy worked in a court of law, where someone's intent can be hard to prove, in the court of public opinion, the feeling was thsat he had gotteh away with murder. Though no one used the term "sociopath," the comments after the news of the verdict described his behavior as the acts of a sociopath.

To illustrate, here are some representative comments from the most recent social media comments I reviewed—virtually all of the posters did not believe he accidentally shot through the door. Rather they took the view that this was a classic case of murder out of jealousy or revenge, after which Pistorius used his lies and money to escape the charge of murder. Some critics even compared him to OJ Simpson, who also killed his ex-wife and got away with murder.

Tons, for instance, had this to say:

Pistorius is the OJ Simpson of South Africa, He is not an actor but surely he passed screening. This legless man was fortunate enough to marry a beautiful woman and enjoy flirting while married. I believed he killed her because she is leaving him and because she couldn't put with his bad behavior as explained by his former girlfriend. OJ Simpson was also fortunate to marry a white woman. She divorced him because he is manipulating and controlling too . . .Both of these killers got away with murder

Terrence considered Pistorius's behavior in the court room all an act. As he noted:

. . .This guy is totally guilty. OP blatantly shot this woman, and put on that bull (sh)(it) act in the court room.

For Rich Rodriguez, Pistorius's actions showed he was immediately in cover up mode after killing his girlfriend. As he observed:

So nowadays an intruder climbs into your bathroom from the outside and locks the door. How is he going to steal anything while being in the crapper.?? In addition, Pistorius had to reach under the bed for the gun and he could not see that Reeva was gone??.. Pistorius knew Reeva was in the bathroom when he went for his gun, and when she wouldn't open the door he shot her. After the murder the first person he calls was his manager or handler and not 911 or the police. An hour after he shot her and after they had their story concocted, they then called the authorities.

Finally, to cite one more comment from Quietlyoutrageous, Pistorius's ntent to kill and cover it up with lies was obvious:

OP- GUILTY AS THEY COME! What a crock of rubbish to think he did not have intent to kill! One shot ok, but anything over 3 shots is intent to kill period! He knew exactly who was in the bathroom, No one in the world is that stupid to not know and if he wasn't some celebrity then he would already be behind bars where he should be!

In sum, though no one used the term "sociopath" in reacting to the Pistorius actions and his trial, the general consensus was that Pistorius acted intentionally and afterwards tried to get out of the responsibility for what he did by claiming a fear of an intruder led to a tragic accident. Those who provided these comments believed he lied to escape the consequences of his actions, just like a sociopath might to get what he wants—in this case, freedom from punishment for his actions. And the strategy worked well, since the verdict was "culpable homicide" instead of murder, and a five-year sentence that could result in as little as ten months in jail, followed by the rest of the sentence served under house arrest. As of this writing, after the prosecutor appealed the verdict of manslaughter, an appeals court of five judges found Pistorius guilty of murder on the grounds that he would have known that shooting through the door would have killed whoever was behind it. The court also found that the original trial did not "take into account all the circumstantial evidence involved in the case, including key police evidence, which was in error." Thus, Pistorius will now go to court to receive a new sentence, which could be as little as 15 years, which is the minimum punishment for murder in South Africa. Potentially, he could still appeal on the basis that his Constitutional rights have been violated, and he is now under house arrest, while awaiting the next step in the process.

Thus, in very different contexts, lying can be used to achieve goals and evade consequences—whether in a work/school environment or in one's personal life, as further illustrated in the following chapters.

CHAPTER 7:
LIVING WITH A SOCIOPATHIC LIAR

Some victims have ended up in a very close relationship with a sociopath. They fall in love, wooed by the sociopath's charm, only to find he or she increasingly becomes a manipulating liar. The honeymoon stage of the relationship ends and the victim realizes they are caught in the sociopath's trap, even though they may not use this term. But whether this personal relationship evolves into living together or in marriage, victims typically don't know this is a problem at first. Rather they become involved in what generally starts off as a friendship or sexual liaison and develops into an increasingly romantic and intimate relationship that turns into regular dating, commitment, and living together. Commonly, the relationship begins with a honeymoon phase, in which the sociopathic partner is on his or her best behavior, being outwardly charming, glib, and personable. Given the sociopath's ability to play the chameleon and act out multiple identities, he or she can readily adapt to become the kind of a desirable mate.

So if you find that a person you have grown close to suddenly transforms after the relationship becomes even closer—and especially after you start living together—that's a clear warning sign. If the person isn't on drugs or experiencing unusual stress that's transforming the personality, he or she could well be a sociopath.

In any event, when a partner lives with a sociopath, the sociopath may use deception and lies to conceal who he or she really is as well as any past history that may put up red flags. As needed, the sociopath can craft an identity to seem like a good fit with the targeted partner. Should any discrepancies be questioned, the sociopath can come up with ready answers to explain these away. And given most people's willingness to trust and not be suspicious of someone who has the right appearance and seems to have the right intentions, a victim can easily fall into the sociopath's trap. In a personal relationship, that can mean falling in love and mistakenly thinking the sociopath feels that way, too.

However, since a characteristic of the sociopath is not feeling emotions or any emotional attachments to others, any sign of falling in love is
part of the charade, which helps to entrap the partner who really is in love
into feeling an even closer relationship with the sociopath. But what might
feel like love to the victim is more like a victory or conquest for the sociopath, who experiences the satisfaction that that he or she can now exercise
even greater control and manipulation over the partner, and using lies as
needed to remain in charge.

So you might consider if you or any family members, friends, or associates are in this kind of situation with a controlling, domineering partner,
and if this is a sociopath, reform is unlikely. A good strategy is to reduce any
losses and get out if you can with no strings attached. But obviously, if there
are children between you, this complicates matters, so being patient and acting as if everything is normal might be the better strategy, until you can do
something otherwise.

The experience of the individuals profiled in this chapter illustrates
what can happen when a victim is drawn into what he or she thinks is
a loving relationship, and the sociopath gets the upper hand. While the
details and level of devastation differ, similar patterns emerge. While
some may question whether these perpetrators of such misery are actually
sociopaths—since they haven't been diagnosed formally by any psychiatrist or other certified practitioner using diagnostic tools—if an individual
exhibits most or all of the classic behaviors of a sociopath, as previously
described, it seems reasonable to classify that person as a sociopath. So
that's what the individuals I interviewed did in considering that the person
they were living with was a sociopath. A common theme was that they
had never been treated so badly by a person after initially being treated so
well. And after the relationship ended, they felt much like a whirlwind had
whooshed through their life, destroying everything in its path.

Now, here are their stories. You can judge for yourself.

Ben: The Innocent Artist

Ben's story is the classic case of a sociopath taking control of a lonely and
vulnerable person and using lies and excuses to keep the relationship
going, until it all falls apart and the victim is left devastated and not fully
understanding what happened.

Ben's relationship with Samantha began hopeful and innocently
enough. He was living in a rural area near St. Louis, where he worked as
a fine arts painter in a barn outside his farm house, which he converted
into a studio. It was filled with several dozen of his paintings, which he
occasionally submitted to gallery shows, and he worked sporadically for
private clients, painting portraits or landscapes. Ben's income varied from

month to month, he had nearly paid off the mortgage, and his elderly parents, who he visited regularly, lived nearby.

However, while he loved his work, he felt lonely, because of his relatively Spartan country existence, and long felt socially awkward among women, since he had always been gangly, thin, and shy. Compounding the problem, his father came down with the early stages of Alzheimer's, so Ben had to regularly check in on his father, besides devoting time to painting for a few hours each day.

Then, he met Samantha on Facebook, when they both commented on some of the funny pictures that popped up on his News Group. After some time and many messages back and forth, Samantha opted to drive to visit him on his farm, claiming to be a student at a nearby university, in the Teacher's Ed program, because she wanted to teach children—a claim that made Ben even more interested in Samantha, since he taught art classes part-time at another local university. And as a future teacher, Samantha helped with his father by reading to him and keeping him entertained, giving Ben more time to paint. Samantha also seemed very impressed by Ben's work, and even volunteered to pose for him.

Soon, Ben was falling hard for her, and he felt Samantha had fallen for him, too. After all, she was driving to see him, about an hour's drive away, three or four times a week. But the first sign of problems came when Samantha told him she needed help with her tuition for her last year at school. He helped her out, although Ben should have become suspicious and checked out Samantha's story. That's because any time there is a request for money early in a relationship, it could mean that the person making the request is building the relationship for financial gain, while leading the victim to feel the relationship is really built on love. It's a classic con game, and sociopaths are really good at it, because they can readily charm and act out any identity. So they start off slowly charming the victim and then asking for money, and later asking for even more.

That's what happened when Samantha made other requests for Ben's help. One time she called him claiming her car broke down about fifty miles outside town, after she told Ben she was headed home from their weekend together. She even had a ready explanation for why she had driven fifty miles in the other direction: She said she had gotten a call to help a long-time friend who had a big fight with her boyfriend. So, at her request, Ben wired her $100 to help get her car fixed.

Soon afterwards, Samantha needed more help for various other reasons, and each time, wanting to believe her, Ben gave her a little cash, since he felt they had such a close, loving relationship.

He even accepted her story after he got a sudden call from a male caller who wanted to know: "Who are you and why is your number on Samantha's phone?"

The man explained that he was calling "Because I'm her husband," then Ben heard signs of a struggle, and a slammed door. Moments later, Samantha was on the phone, trying to keep the relationship going.

"I'm so sorry," she explained. "But my husband and I have been fighting a lot. We're probably getting a divorce, and I didn't want you to know. I thought it might break up our relationship. And you know I love you so much. I'd do anything for you."

So from being surprised and angry at realizing Samantha had lied to him about her marriage, his heart melted at those words, and he felt ready to forgive her.

Then, as he heard the banging on the door again and a man's voice yelling: "Hey, Samantha, don't play games with me," Samantha continued with another story that made her the alleged victim.

"My husband's psycho," she explained. "He's out to kill me. He's beat me up before, and now he's trying to trick me to go back to him."

So the phone call did the trick. Ben forgot about the lies Samantha had told him, and didn't think to question whether Samantha's claims about her dangerous husband were true. He just wanted to help, so he invited her to stay at his place for a while, to which she readily agreed.

The incident was another turning point, when Ben should have questioned the continuing series of lies since the beginning of their relationship to wonder if the supposed fight with her husband was even true, because it could well be part of the set up to suck Ben further into her scheme. But instead, Ben responded emotionally, because of his strong need for companionship and his fear of this being his last opportunity for finding love, given his advancing years.

Later that night, Samantha arrived, but when she unpacked, Ben wondered why she had no books for her teacher's ed program. Samantha had a ready answer—Because her husband wanted her to just be a housewife, she was afraid he might try to destroy her books, so she stored them in a locker at the school.

It was still another lie, but it seemed reasonable at the time, so Ben readily accepted her explanation, especially since he was so glad to see her, and so desperately wanted their relationship to work. It was like Samantha was finally pulling him out of his shell, so he felt liberated and free. But he was leaving himself open and vulnerable, and Samantha demanded more of him. As he began to uncover her lies, Samantha's increasing rage turned against him.

One lie he soon discovered when he ran into an old high school buddy with his university major was that Samantha wasn't enrolled in the teacher's ed program, and the school later confirmed that. When Ben confronted her, she claimed to be auditing some classes, while deciding whether to enroll or not, and Samantha claimed she had to spend money on car repairs rather than for her education. So she decided to audit the classes, and she felt she could learn enough to work in a private school, even if she didn't have a degree.

Ben backed down from more questions, not wanting to provoke an argument, and he let slide some of the other small lies Samantha told, such as when she claimed she had gone shopping in one place but had gone someplace else. Samantha quickly came back with a ready excuse, saying "I forgot," "I was tired," or "I didn't say that. You must have misunderstood."

Ben was also willing to forgive the small lies because he was charmed by the way Samantha seemed to like everything he did, such as when she told him she was eager to learn to paint, and soon began to accompany him to paint in the surrounding countryside. Likewise, she indicated that she liked the same bands he did, and was eager to learn to fish with him. So Samantha was learning how to mirror him, and Ben took that as an example that they were the perfect soul mates, sharing so much in common. Also, he experienced the mirroring as the highest form of flattery, which he much needed, since he lacked self-confidence having never developed a long-term close relationship with a woman. He felt a growing self-assurance because Samantha seemed to so highly value who he was and what he liked. If only he could have put aside his emotions to recognize that this build up was part of the con. Instead, for nine months, Samantha worked him like a fiddle with her string of lies, flattery, and appeals for his financial help.

But finally, after nine months, the honeymoon phase based on pretense came to an end. Now that Samantha had entrapped him, by leading him to think he had found true love, she could manipulate him using more lies and excuses to keep him under her control. For example, she kept reassuring him that the divorce with her psycho husband was going through, although at times she claimed her husband was trying to trick her into coming to see him, because he was jealous she was seeing Ben.

At last now Ben was beginning to question Samantha's stories, although at this point, a skillful sociopath could find other lies to reassure a wavering victim, which is exactly what Samantha did. After Ben shared his concerns with a friend, someone Samantha claimed to know, the friend said he didn't know her at all, and he urged Ben not to trust her. But again Ben held back from confronting Samantha, afraid of triggering an argument, especially when Samantha seemed so sincere in claiming to be very afraid of her husband.

Then, after Samantha briefly got a job as a waitress at a popular night club, Ben learned that Samantha was telling lies about him to her friends at the club, so they wouldn't talk to him. For example, she told them Ben was constantly jealous around her, hitting her, and reneging on his promise to help her get a degree in education, when none of this was true.

When Ben finally tried to call Samantha on her lies, she responded with a variety of strategies, as sociopaths often do when confronted. They try different approaches to see what works, like a marketer testing different marketing campaigns. They usually have no emotional investment in a particular strategy—they just want to sell whatever they are selling.

So now Samantha was selling Ben on believing her to keep the relationship going, one approach was to accuse Ben of being wrong, saying she didn't do what others said she did. They were liars, she asserted, trying to get her in trouble with Ben. Another strategy was to become very apologetic in asking for Ben's forgiveness, and then "love bombing" him by being extra nice, such as baking him some treat or pulling him into bed and making passionate love. Still another approach was telling Ben a more serious lie, such as the time she said she was pregnant and the doctor said she needed extra rest. But when Ben called the clinic the next day to check her story, due to his growing suspicions, the clinic had no record of her ever being a patient.

When Ben reported back what he had discovered—that her clinic story was a lie—Samantha played the "pity me" approach, a strategy sociopaths sometimes use when they are about to be unmasked. To gain pity, Samantha explained that she was sick, and needed Ben's help to overcome her propensity to make up stories, since she wanted so badly for the two of them to be together and she was so afraid to lose him.

Certainly, at this point, Ben should have realized Samantha was just telling more lies, but he was completely unaware of a sociopath's tactics to deny and then seek pity, so he remained stuck in the trap. But if you are aware of such methods, you can know when to cut your losses and get out.

But Ben did not, so he agreed to help Samantha, and at first she agreed to go to a support group to get help. But after the group leader told him she didn't show up a few times, Ben insisted he would go with her and did so. After the therapist spoke to them together and separately, he warned Ben that Samantha was "crying wolf." So he urged Ben to draw some boundaries to make it clear what was acceptable behavior, which included her telling him the truth. That's when Samantha began getting violent and vengeful, as if to show she was still the boss in the relationship, and if Ben wouldn't accept her stories, she was going to make him pay. According to Ben:

> "As soon as I drew boundaries, she began getting violent and jealous. She started hitting me, as if trying to get me to hit her back, but I would just leave. Several times when I tried to leave, she jumped on my back and pounded on me, while I walked out the door. One time she held a knife to my dog's throat and threatened to kill him if I left, so I listened as she yelled at me about all the things I did wrong."

Unfortunately, Ben didn't recognize her actions as the end game for a sociopath—seeking revenge after they get thwarted and realize the victim is likely on his or her way out. So instead, Ben stayed in this volatile situation, in part because Samantha played on his need to be loved and needed. After she calmed down from these rages, she pled, "I'm sick, and I need your help," so he would feel he needed to help. Then, in these periods of calm, Samantha would "love bomb" him, again trying to be nice and loving, as in the beginning, or she would lead him to question his experience, that he was accusing her for something she didn't do.

Thus, Ben kept hoping things would get better if Samantha got the help she needed, but instead the cycle of lies and excuses, leading to more arguments and violence, would start again. Meanwhile, Ben found it difficult to pursue his own work, since he was spending so much time trying to help Samantha. And even when he got her a couple of jobs, she didn't show up, despite her claims of going to work. Then, when Ben confronted her, she played her sick card: "Please, help."

So, things kept getting worse. "The cycles between when she was nice and loving and when she sought to get back at me happened more quickly," Ben said.

Plus now she began hiding things and breaking things.

But finally Ben came to a turning point, as many sociopath victims often do when they finally realize things aren't going to change and it's not their own fault, but the nature of the sociopath. As Ben described one especially dramatic incident that led him to decide it was the end of the relationship.

"I was watching the *Royal Tenenbaums* on TV, which is a drama about a dysfunctional upper class family. When Samantha came into the room, she said she wouldn't allow pornography in her house and then left the room. A few minutes later, I found her in the bathroom with a bottle of whiskey and pills, which I pulled away from her. Then, she fled out of the house into the woods with my phone and drove away. But I couldn't go after her, since she had hidden my keys. She came back about five hours later, saying she was very sorry, and gave me back my keys and the phone. She said she wasn't committing suicide. She was just very upset and was trying to calm herself down."

This incident was the final breakthrough Ben needed, since he realized that Samantha's biggest lie was that she was sick. "But she wasn't sick. It's what she did when what she was doing wasn't working. Every time I would confront one of her lies, she would use illness to get away."

Yet, while Ben had finally woken up to the truth about his relationship built on a foundation of lies, it was not so easy to break away, because

Samantha didn't want to let him go, like a predator with its prey. She wanted to hang on as long as she could or get revenge, for having been found out and being pushed out. Again, this is what sociopaths often do: they act like a wild animal cornered in a trap and they fight back ferociously to attack the trapper and get away.

For example, at first she refused to leave, saying she had nowhere to go, and he couldn't just kick her out at will, since this had been her home So he had to give her thirty days' notice, send an eviction notice, and ask the sheriff to force her out, if she still refused to leave. Meanwhile, as Ben waited it out, Samantha packed her suitcases but didn't leave, which made it increasingly tough for him. She repeatedly hid his things, like his car keys, so he had to waste time looking for them, and he found broken dishes around the house, like a "don't mess with me" message from Samantha.

Still Ben was determined to end things, and after Samantha did get the eviction notice, she prepared to go. But as she walked out, she left Ben with the threat that "I'm going to ruin you, because of the way you treated me."

At last, seeing her drive away with her suitcases in the back seat, Ben thought she was finally gone for good, but he soon found out that wasn't true, as he tried to pull his life back together.

Back in the house, he found handwritten Post-It notes from Samantha all over the house, with messages threatening that terrible things would happen to him. In one, she hoped that Ben would "soon be found dead or paralyzed from a car crash, so you can never paint again." In another she wrote that "I love you, but I just can't control myself."

Then, he discovered she had taken his list of friends on Facebook and told them that Ben had abandoned her or was mentally disturbed. But the worst was yet to come. Ben discovered that Samantha had broken his three computers and had taken the hard drives, which contained over ten years of work, including both drawings and completed paintings. Also on these drives were about 600 albums of music that he had been collecting since he was a child. But there was little he could do, because the police said it was a civil matter, because Samantha had taken what she did while she was living with him. Plus they warned that if she did return the hard drives, they might have nothing on them, and he would have no way to prove that she had stolen or destroyed his work.

But it seemed like Samantha had an even more devious reason for stealing his portfolio beyond trying to ruin Ben—to reinvent herself from a teacher to an artist, using his work. As Ben discovered, Samantha was once married to an elementary school teacher and adopted key aspects of his persona in claiming to be a teacher in training. Then, he discovered that she had created a website in which she described herself as a painter, and even posted some of his early paintings. Plus she listed some of her favorite musical artists, which were the same ones featured on his hard drive. Such actions in adopting this information about Ben for herself is in keeping with what a sociopath might do in creating a new identity because of a lack of their own core self. Sociopaths steal the persona of their victims.

In turn, this theft of one's identity can be devastating for the victim. Just think how you might feel if you find someone is traveling around the country who had stolen your identity via the web and was now posing as you or claiming your hard-earned work or credentials as her own. Well, that's how Ben felt. He was appalled at what he had discovered, feeling that he had been literally violated and stripped of his identity by Samantha. As he described it:

"I felt like she took my identity. Now she claimed to be an artist, a painter, and she was showing off some of my paintings and was claiming to like the music I did. It was like a personal attack on me and everything I used to define myself."

Though he wanted to fight back, on the advice of a cop, his lawyer, and a therapist, he decided it was best to walk away rather than prolong a battle he couldn't win with someone who could easily move on and take on still another name and identity. Yet, even though the relationship was ended, Samantha was not quite ready to let everything go, since she still sought to intimidate Ben and show him she was still in charge.

Needless to say, the experience left Ben feeling devastated, like a tornado had swept through his life, creating chaos and mixing up everything he once held dear. At one time everything had seemed so perfect, like he and Samantha were soul mates who shared so many interests. But once he was caught in the relationship, Samantha changed and went from trying to control and manipulate him to trying to undermine and destroy him. And to a great extent she did succeed, because as Ben spent more time at the end of the relationship trying to deal with her claims of illness, he had less time for his own work. As a result, many of his own painting commissions dried up, plus the economy made it more difficult for artists in general. Then, when he sought to arrange to show his work in galleries, he couldn't, because he no longer had the hard drive featuring ten years of his work.

So now Ben is still trying to rebuild his life with the help of his therapist, though he feels he will be forever wary when it comes to love and trust again, after being once burnt so badly. He was willing to stay in a toxic relationship for so long, because he thought he had finally found true love and Samantha played on his need for that. He "didn't want to spoil it," although clearly once he experienced Samantha's continuous lies, he should have pulled back and he should not have fallen for her "pity me" routine. He had a genuine desire to help others, and Samantha took advantage of that. Her plight wasn't real, but she made Ben think it was. She found this was a vulnerability of his.

Likewise, should you feel someone is trying to take advantage of you, pay attention. Don't let them dissuade you from your gut level feeling that something is wrong, because it could very well be. And if you know you have certain weaknesses and vulnerabilities, be especially sensitive when someone seeks to appeal to that, such as when Ben let his desire to be loved and his desire to help overcome his good sense, which would have led him to doubt Samantha's excuses and explanations.

What motivated Samantha to seek out Ben and react so violently to get revenge, when he began to confront her lies and the relationship ended? While one can only speculate, perhaps a reason is Ben's vulnerability that drew him and led him to fall so passionately in love. She saw his weakness, so she could easily move into his life and take charge, using lies to build his love and trust, which is what sociopaths in relationships do. Without any feeling or conscience, with only the desire to dominate and win, they can easily put on a mask to become what they sense the other person wants them to be. Moreover, when Samantha met Ben she was at the end of a marriage that was breaking up, so Ben might have seemed like a safe harbor where she could go once the relationship with her husband ended, and a place she especially needed, because she had no training to get a good job to support herself.

And so the relationship with Ben began. Then, the more Ben became passionately in love with her, the more her own interest in the game with him began to wane, much like a victor moves on after one conquest to the next. Even so, she continued to use lies to keep him in line, including the mental illness pity ploy towards the end. And for a time her appeal to pity worked. But once Ben began to question and distrust her even more, she turned against him, which is unfortunately often the result in personal relationships with sociopaths, who can charm in the beginning, then attack and destroy with little remorse, before moving on to the next victim.

Thus, it can be important to prepare for any fallout on ending a relationship with a sociopath. Besides participating in counseling or a support group to help you hold up emotionally to withstand any vengeful actions, consider ways to avoid future contact, such as the sociopath's ploys to see you again, which could turn ugly, once the sociopath realizes the relationship really is over and he or she has lost control of you. Sometimes it may even be necessary to seek the help of police or other protection after you first make the break, which is when the sociopath is most likely to feel rage and seek revenge.

Cherise: Caught in a Family of Sociopaths

The following experience by Cherise illustrates the same kind of pattern of creating what seems to be a good relationship at first but then turns ugly and violent.

Cherise's story also raises some questions about the nature of becoming a sociopath. Can becoming a sociopath be due to genetic influences? Or does the environment in which one is raised play a part? Cherise's story addresses these issues, because her husband Terrence was raised in a family of doctors and some nurses, who followed the family patriarch's medical tradition. They also showed the classic traits of a sociopath—such as no conscience, a lack of empathy and emotion, a determination to win at all costs, and frequently lying to support this behavior.

For Cherise, then twenty-eight, the descent into the crazy-making world of the sociopath began when she went to work in the medical practice of Jarod, the family patriarch, where Terrence, thirty-seven, also worked. She and Terrence got to talking during lunch and coffee breaks in the office kitchen, and soon she felt a strong emotional and physical attraction to him. As Cherise described it:

"It was like we were soul mates. Whatever I liked, he liked the same thing. Movies, food, ideal vacation spots. It didn't matter. If I mentioned really liking something, he did, too. So I felt this strong connection, like we were meant to be together; like he completed me.

Though several other girls who worked as receptionists warned Cherise about getting involved with Terrence, telling her "He's not what he seems," she ignored their warnings. She felt they were just jealous. When one of the women told her that Terrence got her pregnant and she gave the child up for adoption, she wanted to believe Terrence when he admitted everything, and explained that he had given up his younger, wilder ways.

So Cherise was willing to forgive and forget, when he assured her that she was the only one for him now. After that, for a few weeks, Cherise felt very much cherished and loved, since Terrence put her on a pedestal by praising her highly, telling her how smart she was, and repeatedly saying how much he loved and cared for her.

But his words were all a sham, as Cherise soon found out after she got pregnant and according to Cherise, "He was horrible to me."

For one thing, she discovered Terrence was still secretly dating three other women, when she found their phone and email messages at the clinic, and none of the women knew about the others. When he took her to a restaurant for dinner, she confronted him about the women. Though at first Terrence denied it and accused the woman of lying, Cherise persisted, telling him about the messages. Likewise, he firmly denied it when

Cherise told him she had heard about a second employee who had gotten pregnant and had an abortion.

"I would never support that, since I'm very pro-life," he claimed.

When Cherise said she had seen the woman's receipts from the clinic, he admitted it, but tried to smooth things over with the excuse: "I didn't want to lose you by telling you this. And since this happened, I found God. I reformed myself."

Then, to cast blame for his actions, as sociopaths often do, he told Cherise that he had trouble fending off the many women who threw themselves at him.

"They all wanted to marry me, since I'm a doctor. But they were psychos and not right for me. Then I found you, and you're perfect."

Thinking Terrence meant all he said about being reformed and ready to commit himself only to her, Cherise forgave him. But that was just the beginning of a growing series of lies and actions to take advantage of her feelings for him. Much like Ben, Cherise followed her heart, not her head, because she wanted the relationship to succeed so much. However, once a relationship gets filled with lies, that's a time to consider that it's time to end it and move on, unless you see real changes in the other person's actions, not just what he or she says to explain away secrets and discrepancies. Just claims that someone is changing are not enough, since sociopaths generally don't change at all; they just claim they have or will.

That's what happened in Cherise's case. After she ignored the warning signs, wanting to trust, and forgave Terrance, soon after that his effort to take advantage of her began again and again. As an example, Terrence asked Cherise to help him finance a car, saying he needed one for his work at the clinic. But he couldn't afford it himself, since he was struggling and the clinic, his father owned was going bankrupt. So his father couldn't finance the car either. At first, Cherise said no, concerned about loaning several thousand dollars, but Terrence was persuasive, telling her they would be married soon, so it was only natural for the partners to share what they had. He even had his father call her to pressure her to give Terrence her credit card information for the loan. So finally, reluctantly, Cherise gave in, and Terrence got the car, though later she learned he frequently used it to impress other women. And while he used some of the money for a down payment on the loan, he used the rest—several thousand dollars—to pay his bookie, so he could gamble on college football games, but over time he lost the funds.

Then, a month before the baby was due, they got married. But as much as Cherise was glad for the coming baby, she felt increasingly trapped in a relationship, in which Terrence became more and more controlling. When his parents moved to the same city, she felt even more trapped. It was like Terrence now had reinforcements in his efforts to control her to do his bidding, while treating her more like a servant than as a wife.

For example, after Cherise returned to work, the head of the clinic, under the direction of Terrence's father, instructed her to come in through the back entrance; not in the front entrance anymore. When she complained about this change in policies, Terrence warned of dire consequences from his father. So rather than provoke a confrontation, Cherise meekly complied.

Then, she experienced a series of put-downs when Terrence brought in Christmas gifts for the other employees, but didn't have a gift for her, so she felt embarrassed in front of her co-workers. When she asked him about it, he answered coldly: "I'm the employer; I can do what I want with the other staff members. It's none of your business."

Another problem was that Terrence continued to gamble, despite struggling financially, engaging in the risky behavior for stimulation which is characteristic of sociopaths. He told more lies to keep the behavior from her, but in a few weeks, she found out when unpaid bill notices arrived.

More problems developed when she had her child. Terrence insisted that she should keep the child's birth a secret from the rest of the family, because his father didn't want to acknowledge the child. He still hadn't fully accepted Cherise's marriage to him, and Terrence wanted to keep the peace.

Cherise also found herself up against Terrence and his family's resistance to hospital care, since they practiced natural medicine using herbs and natural remedies. So when her daughter Leila became ill, she resorted to lying and secrecy herself to obtain the medical treatment she felt was necessary. She hid Leila's medicine in her friend's refrigerator and took Leila to see a doctor for a high fever, instead of relying on the natural medicine the rest of the family preferred. As a result, when Terrence found out, he knocked Cherise over and wouldn't pay her doctor's bills. So Cherise had to do some extra part-time work to pay for that, and when Terrence found out, he was furious. He felt Cherise had gone behind his back. Yet when he did something in secret, such as gambling and seeing other women, that was okay.

"He could lie to me, but it wasn't okay for me to lie to him," Cherise said.

In other words, Terrence was angered by anything that Cherise did to assert her independence, since he wanted to manipulate her to do what he wanted. He, however, was free to live outside the laws himself, a classic example of a sociopath's need to control and lie as necessary to stay in charge.

Later, Terrence sought to pull Cherise into the world of swinging and nudism, which was a regular practice of his father. Yet, Cherise resisted, because she was a practicing Christian and felt such acts were immoral. She refused to go or bring their daughter, now six.

Cherise also felt helpless to go outside the family for help, since they had so much power, because Terrence's father had a large following at the church in LA. Cherise felt even more helpless to do anything after she saw some images of boys masturbating in a file on a computer at the clinic. When she spoke to an attorney, he urged her not to do or say anything, since Terrence's family had connections with people in the local government. When she told Terrence what she had seen, he just shrugged his shoulders. He didn't care. He knew his father had unusual sexual urges, but that didn't bother him. According to Cherise, "Terrence told me to shut up about it, or he would have to do something to keep me quiet or discredit anything I tried to do."

At this point, Cherise probably should have left, gotten an opinion from another attorney, perhaps in another town, or at least stayed away from Terrence's father. But Cherise stayed and did nothing, trying to act like everything was normal.

But Terrence made more attempts to control her and dismiss her feelings. One time was when Cherise's father died and she got a phone call about it at the clinic. Terrence showed little concern and told her to go back to work. It was one more example of his lack of emotion and empathy, and Cherise felt more isolated and alone than ever. Then, when she asked Terrence to accompany her to her father's funeral, he turned her down using a lie that his father didn't want him to go, but it was really his way of getting out of doing something he didn't want to do.

Finally, all the pressure and lies became too much. She *had* to get out. But after she left, both Terrence and his father sought to make her life with her daughter miserable. For example, Terrence spread the word among Cherise's employees and other associates that she had shirked her duties as a wife at home because she didn't cook or clean and mistreated him.

"But I did all of that," Cherise said, "and I did yard work. Then, I found out that through much of our marriage, Terrence had been having an affair with a masseuse."

When Terrence enticed her to come to his condo to talk about things, she thought he meant the custody arrangements and visitation. But instead he handed her bills for their daughter's vaccinations. When she claimed he was responsible for these bills, he tried to throw her down and hit her. But she escaped with her daughter. As they ran, he yelled after her that if she reported anything to the police, he would report her for abusing her daughter. Then, he got other family members to describe her as an unfit mother, and she had to fight their lies in court to keep her daughter.

As a result of all of these experiences both in and after the marriage, Cherise developed a deep depression, where she had nightmares, couldn't sleep, and stopped eating, until her weight plummeted to eighty-seven pounds. Though finally, seeing a psychiatrist helped her realize that

Terrence was an evil self-centered man who tried to control her when they were together, and then sought to destroy her now that he was apart from her and had his daughter. She also spent eight days in a hospital to restore her health, due to her huge weight loss, and regain her sanity.

For a time, when Cherise was in the hospital and left her daughter in safe-keeping with friends, Terrence was able to recapture his daughter, Leila, by tricking her friend into letting him inside. Then he escaped with Leila to a waiting car and sped away, hid her, and told the courts that Cherise had abandoned her. But Cherise felt his effort to get her daughter was more to take Leila away from her, rather than because he really wanted Leila for himself, and because he wanted to get out of paying child support. So, eventually, after Cherise's lawyer offered Terrence joint custody and no child support, he dropped his claim and seemed uninterested in caring for Leila.

Yet, while Cherise was now physically free of Terrence, the mental havoc he caused her remained, since the memories of different ways he had manipulated, tricked, or lied to her still plagued her. For example, she began to discover some of the things he had hidden from her, such as when she found $1,700 in bills hidden in Terrence's shoes in his closet. As a result of these discoveries and haunting memories, she felt that the entire world she had known, the very foundations, were all caving in, and she was helpless and lost. Terrence added to her confusion by suggesting she just was mistaken in what she remembered, and she recalled how he had previously confused her. As Cherise explained:

"Terrence had told a lot of stories which weren't true, and many times when I referred to something, he would say 'You just imagined this. You just think you heard that, but you didn't.'

"At the time, I would think, 'okay, I've been mistaken.' But then, as I began to realize there were so many lies, I didn't know what was true and what was not. It was terrible, and I thought I would lose my mind."

So now Cherise had to confront these questions of what was real or not. At this point, Cherise might have consulted a psychologist or psychiatrist specializing in cognitive and neurological issues, much like anyone with such issues should see a specialist to help them identify what is real and what is delusion. But she did not, which contributed to her continuing mental distress.

Later, after Terrence had lost control over Cherise and Leila through the divorce and family courts, he continued to go after Cherise in other ways, unable to let her go. Among other things, he gained access to her phone by hacking into it to see what she was doing, though she repeatedly tried to block him. He followed her on the Internet, too, wherever her name appeared. The experience was unsettling, as Cherise noted, comparing him to a vampire:

> "It's like he's a parasite, trying to not only control me, but find out and take advantage of everything I do. So he feeds on that.
>
> "When we were together, I realized now how he was just like a vampire, feeding on my doing what he wanted and praising him to the skies. And now I think he kept putting me down, so I wouldn't have the confidence to resist him and try to find someone else.
>
> "But since I broke free, it's like he still wants me back in his trap. So that's why he's still coming after me to show me he's still the boss."

Several years later, after having concluded that Terrence was a sociopath, as well as narcissist, Cherise came to believe he was part of a family of sociopaths, with a trait passed down from his father to his children. For example, she found that his father constantly feigned all sorts of things to get what he wanted, such as pretending to be concerned when his best friend's wife was dying of cancer, and he became a frequent hospital visitor, though he hadn't been close to the friend before. Then, shortly before the wife died, he got her and the friend to sign over their life savings to his college, an action Terrence praised highly.

Given her lingering trauma, Cherise finally found it helpful to go into therapy, which is a good idea for anyone experiencing such an ordeal. Living in a relationship with a sociopath can lead one to feel a loss of self-identity and lack of self-confidence, along with self-blame for getting taken in by a sociopath and his or her lies. Also, a support group for victims of sociopaths is recommended, which can help the victims regain that confidence and feel good about themselves again.

That's what happened for Cherise. After many weeks of therapy, her therapist supported her view, pointing out that she had experienced a kind of Post-Stress Traumatic Disorder (PSTD), because not only had she endured the sociopathic behavior from her ex-husband, but from his father and brothers, who supported each other, like the troops in a war. Thus, she had become something of a casualty of the battle, though with her therapist's help, she was trying to pull herself together and protect her daughter from further onslaughts. Still, the experience left her feeling very much alone, since she now found it difficult to trust or relate to others. She was afraid of being caught again in a sociopath's trap, though that is a time when therapy can help by showing ways of learning to trust and love again, while feeling safe.

Trudy: Afraid to Leave a Dangerous Relationship

Sometimes victims get so sucked into a relationship that they feel dependent and they are then afraid to leave. The story of Trudy, in her mid-fifties, is a good example of that. As she told me, she had a boyfriend who became a live-in partner who lied about everything from the time she met him to the very end. She kept believing him until it was almost too late, and she realized she was being set up to be killed so he could go on effortlessly to the next woman. As Trudy told me:

"When I first met Jim in a restaurant in New York, he was very nice, but after a few months, he began to lie about everything, and he always had an explanation if I asked him about anything. For instance, he lied about his family and initially claimed he had two previous wives, instead of three, and . . .

"He also claimed he did restaurant consulting and had inherited a restaurant in New York, though he was stealing money from his mother's credit card to take me out. Later, I found out he stole $80,000 from his mother to pay off an ex-wife."

What led Trudy to stay with him after these discoveries? One reason is that whenever she suspected something was wrong and asked Jim for more information, he got support for his lies from friends and relatives who knew his claims weren't true but backed him up. For example, when Trudy met Jim's mother, she played along when he said he had two wives and three children, although his mother knew about the third wife and child, because she didn't want to face Jim's anger if she contradicted him. When Trudy did some checking in the beginning, she found that Jim had created a web presence that backed up his story, though it listed incorrect information, such as listing places where he had worked, when he hadn't worked there. And should anyone ask for a referral, he was prepared to call on a friend to give a reference.

Trudy also stayed for so long because everything seemed so good in the very beginning. She didn't realize that Jim was using this honeymoon period to make her increasingly dependent on him and isolated from others, much like a cult leader might pull in followers and separate them from their family and friends they have known and trusted in the past. As Trudy described it:

"In the beginning it was very romantic. For example, a few weeks after we met and were living together, he would bring home little gifts for me, and he would offer to do all kinds of things for me, which seemed like really generous, nice gestures, but they made me dependent on him for everything. As an example, though I was used to driving my own car, he would drive me around. Or he would shop and do errands for me. So little by little, I did less, and he increasingly separated me from others, by not wanting to go to events, so I didn't go."

Another strategy Jim used to undermine Trudy's belief in herself and set up a basis for claiming she was unstable should she make any future claims against him is the technique of gaslighting. The strategy got its name from the 1938 stage play *Gaslight* later adapted into a film in 1940 and 1944, in which a husband convinces a wife she is insane by manipulating small elements of their environment. Later he claims she is mistaken or has remembered incorrectly when she points out these changes. Since the 1970s, the term has been used to describe efforts to manipulate someone's sense of reality.

That's what Trudy realized that Jim had been doing to her. For example, one time he called his mother several times to tell her that something was wrong with Trudy and that she was threatening to kill herself. When his mother called, Trudy downplayed Jim's claim by saying it was just an argument, and when his mother asked Jim about it, he told her Trudy was trying to start a fight, because she was menopausal and should see a doctor. So Trudy, wanting to keep the peace, backed away from a confrontation, while these repeated experiences led her to increasingly doubt herself. Eventually, though, she began to realize that Jim was using this technique to show that she was becoming mentally ill and suicidal, should something happen to her. At the same time, he was setting up the next woman to take her place. As Trudy explained:

"Everything changed after 1½ years, when we planned to go to New Mexico, where I hoped to open up a yoga studio. So he went out ahead of me, while I sold the house. During this time, he called me frequently, to make sure I was still in New York and not going to New Mexico to surprise him, since, as I learned later, he was seeing many other women.

"At the same time, while he was telling me about all the great couples he had met there, he was planting seeds to all these people that I was a horrible person, who was doing terrible things, going crazy, and becoming suicidal.

"Then, one night he attacked and beat me up for 1½ hours. I tried to rationalize this away by thinking his drinking led him to become violent. So I tried to downplay the incident when I went to hospital. But after the nurses saw the injuries, they reported it to the police, who arrested him and put him on probation. So I was safe from further attacks.

"After that, I really became afraid of him, when he suggested we should get away from it all and rekindle our romance and I found camping equipment and a machete in his truck. Though claimed the machete was there in case anything attacked us, I became very afraid of him. I thought back to everything else that happened and felt he was trying to set me up, so he could claim I was becoming crazy, suicidal, and just disappeared."

Finally things ended, with Trudy realizing that Jim was not all that he seemed to be and that he was setting her up to be killed. For many victims, such a realization about the sociopath's hostility is devastating. It is like they have been living in an unreal world, since the sociopath has led them to believe what the sociopath wants, while making them dependent and taking advantage of the victim in various ways. For many, the separation is far more traumatic than any other kind of romantic breakup, because it is like coming out of living in a cult that has redefined the nature of reality and created new bonds and dependencies within the group that are very hard to break, until reality hits. As Trudy explained:

"When things end with a sociopath, it is not like any other breakup. You don't understand what happened. You feel like the life you have known is unreal, and the relationship has undermined your sense of self identity. You feel like the sociopath has stolen your soul, like your spirit is broken."

Then, as often happens with sociopaths, they go on from one victim to repeat the pattern with another, as happened with Jim. According to Trudy, he went to Arizona where he hooked up with another woman, but she left him after she saw the light. He was homeless for a while, and finally returned to live with his mother in New York.

As for the victims, once a relationship ends and the victim realizes how he or she has been victimized, the victim has to go through an extensive healing process, with the experience leaving the victim reluctant to trust again. For example, Trudy said she was only willing to date people she has met through a friend; she would no longer date someone she has just met without having a personal connection, which was how she met Jim at a restaurant.

Should you see such a pattern like this developing in your own relationship, it's probably good to get out quickly and cut off further communication with the sociopath best you can.

Living with the Lies of a Sociopath

As these stories illustrate, in these relationships with a sociopath, the beginning is like a courtship and honeymoon, which involves the victim in thinking this a wonderful relationship. The sociopath may indicate liking whatever the victim likes, so they seem to share the same interests. The victim may even feel the sociopath is a soul mate, drawing him or her even more closely into the sociopath's web. But unfortunately, once the victim is hooked, the sociopath may start taking advantage of the victim in various ways, such as borrowing money or getting special favors The victim's altruism and willingness to help opens the door to further victimization, rather than the sociopath's true appreciation. On the surface, the sociopath may seem grateful, but he or she views the victim's assistance as a sign of being vulnerable to further victimization. In a personal relationship, this victimization can be even more devastating emotionally than when the sociopath victimizes someone in a work or business setting, though often the business and personal gets mixed, as described in the stories in the next chapter.

A common pattern, shown in these stories, is that once the victim is pulled in, the sociopath's behavior changes, so increasingly the exterior charm that pulled in the victim is replaced by actions to control the victim, using lies and other means to get what the sociopath wants. Later, if the victim confronts the sociopath over any actions or lies or seeks to leave the relationship, the sociopath may be out for revenge.

For example, as we've seen with Ben, the lonely artist, his first experience with Samantha seemed as if she was someone who shared many interests with him, was very interested in his work, and was willing to drive for hours each way to see him. Then, increasingly, he discovered things she was covering up or fabricating, such as a husband she was still married to and not being a student in a degree program like she said. Also, Ben was bombarded by even more deception, including Samantha's lie that she was trying to recover from a mental illness, "so pity me." Finally, when it was clear things weren't working and Ben wanted out, Samantha turned vicious. First, she wouldn't leave until he threatened to evict her, and after she moved out, she stole his hard drive with his life's work, claiming the work on his hard drive as her own.

Similarly, Cherise fell very hard for Terrence when she began work as a receptionist in his father's medical practice. But once she fell in love with him, she began to discover his cheating followed by his cover-ups, promises to reform, and more lies. Still, she was hopeful enough to marry him. However, once married, she experienced an increasing number of indignities, such as being forced to come to the office through the back door and seeing Terrence give gifts to the other employees, but not her. Worse, she had to fight off Terrence's efforts to pull her and her child into what she considered a sinful world of swinging and nudity. Later, once

Cherise was determined to leave and hold onto her child, she experienced the wrath of Terrence and his father, who sought to make her life miserable. Terrence not only falsely shamed her as an unfit mother with the clinic employees where she once worked, but he became physically abusive when she came to his condo thinking they would talk about custody arrangements. He even stole her daughter away for a time while she was in the hospital.

Likewise, Trudy was initially swept off her feet by Jim, though later, when the relationship soured, he tried to make it seem that Trudy was mentally ill and even suicidal, which could be a way of setting her up to get rid of her.

Another similar pattern is that these cases left the victims feeling very traumatized and damaged. Trudy was homeless for a while as she struggled to get back on her feet, while Ben and Cherise had to see therapists after their relationships ended to overcome their emotional trauma due to the upheaval in their lives caused by their life with a sociopath. Meanwhile, without any conscience or emotional feelings, and fueled by the sociopaths' desire to win, control, and achieve their objectives, Ben and Cherise's one-time partners felt free to go after their next victim.

In short, their stories illustrate the common stages in the relationships with sociopaths, which all are characterized by different types of lies that help the sociopath entrap the victim, manipulate, take advantage of, and finally seek revenge when the victim tries to leave the relationship. Later after the victim does escape, the sociopath may still be unwilling to let the victim go. The four phases are these:

1. The initial wooing and honeymoon phase.
2. The ongoing relationship where the sociopath seeks to manipulate and control the victim through a mix of enticements and efforts to undermine the victim's confidence and sense of self.
3. The breakdown of the relationship to where the victim increasingly seeks to confront the sociopath about their hurtful actions and lies.
4. The end of the relationship, marked by the sociopath's anger and efforts to get revenge, and sometimes seek to reconcile or maintain contact, thereby restarting the cycle.

So what should you do if you start seeing any of these patterns develop in a relationship?

1. Learn more about who the person is. See if you can meet any people who have met, worked with, or been in a relationship before with that person.
2. Early on, discuss your concerns with your partner to see if he or she responds with lies. If so, this is an early warning sign that you can't fully

trust this person, and if you find yourself facing more and more lies, it's time to consider seriously ending the relationship. Trust is at the foundation of any good relationship, while lies are part of the sociopath's *modus operandi*. And in very many relationships with sociopaths, problems escalate, and things don't end well.

CHAPTER 8:

HAVING A WORK AND PERSONAL RELATIONSHIP WITH A SOCIOPATH

While some individuals only encounter a sociopath in their workplace, usually as a boss or co-worker, some find that the relationship includes both the workplace and their personal life. This mixture can occur because the person starts working with the sociopath and that blossoms into a romantic relationship, which sometimes leads to marriage, or because individuals in a social relationship start a business together. In these mixed work and personal situations, the havoc resulting from the relationship can be even worse and more emotionally devastating. The following stories illustrate how these different types of personal-work relationships with a sociopath can go south.

A Woman Whose Husband Took Over the Business

Sandra's story shows how a sociopath can not only victimize his partner in a marriage and business, but the clients of the business, while achieving great financial success. As typical with sociopaths, Sandra's relationship of twenty-five years with her sociopathic husband began with a lot of wooing to attract her into marriage and then into a business partnership running an art gallery in Los Angeles.

It all began when Sandra, then twenty-five, worked at a gallery after graduating from college, where she had majored in art history. Alex, twenty-seven, who later became her husband and business partner, worked in the office as the gallery's accountant. Soon the two were not only dating, but Alex wanted the freedom gained from starting their own gallery. Since they were so young, they got an older partner to front for them.

At first the business arrangement seemed perfect. Sandra, with her art history background, selected the artists and arranged the shows, while Alex wrote up the contracts, negotiated with the artists, and established the pricing for customers. Plus, Alex did the accounting as he had at the gallery where they met. After a few years of jointly running the new gallery, they also got married, although the business remained the main focus.

Yet, while everything started off well enough, Sandra began to find that some of Alex's underhanded sales, contract, and other business practices bothered her. For example, in the interest of making more money, Alex would lie and break promises to the artists in order to pay them less. He also lied to get more money from customers, such as if someone expressed interest in an art piece but was reluctant to buy because of the price or other reason. To fuel their eagerness to buy now, Alex would tell them customers that someone was coming in the next day to buy the piece, even though no one expressed such interest, and the strategy often resulted in a sale at the price asked.

Initially, Sandra put her observations about Alex's deceptive business practices aside, since they contributed to the gallery's success, and after two years, she and Alex set up the partnership on their own, without a third party front anymore. By the third year, they were doing so well that they opened additional galleries in other parts of L.A.

But that's when, according to Sandra, "things started becoming weird." She noticed more and more examples of Alex's lies and deceptions, and she felt increasingly uncomfortable at being pulled into this web of broken promises, misrepresentation, and fraud. As Sandra explained it:

> "I started to notice things as a partner that were wrong, because he was breaking promises or misstating things to suppliers, artists, clerks, and customers. For example, at times, he would promise things to people, such as giving them a special deal or paying them a referral to bring us a new customer. But then, he would tell people he didn't say that and they must have heard him incorrectly. Or he would promise the artists a certain percent for a sale. but then he wouldn't pay them that much, and he would tell them he hadn't made that promise. He also kept a second set of records and books and gave the artist a fake invoice, so the artist would receive half of the promised percentage. When I said something to him about it, Alex got very mad and yelled at me, saying: 'What team are you on?' So I backed off, but the deception bothered me."

Unfortunately, backing off just gave Alex more space to continue the deception, as if Sandra was giving her tacit consent. Instead, she should have told Alex she couldn't be a party to such deceptions, and she should be willing to accept the end of their partnership and even their marriage. If not, it was as if she was going along with a fraud by looking the other way while knowing about it. And his actions now were a sign that things would get worse, because his deceptions were likely to continue.

Meanwhile, as things deteriorated in their business partnership, Sandra noticed more and more patterns of sociopathic behavior in Alex, though she didn't call it that at the time, and things began to go sour in their marriage, too.

One big change occurred when Sandra had to stop working and rest in bed because of her pregnancy with their first child. Alex decided she should no longer sleep in the master bedroom with him, since she was so heavy. Then after the baby was born, he didn't want her in the bedroom with the baby either, because he was disturbed by the baby's cries or by Sandra getting up to feed the baby. So, Sandra slept with the kids for 5½ years.

Meanwhile, more lies and deceptions occurred when he began seeing other women, and using a variety of ploys and ever changing stories to keep them secret from Sandra, such as claiming a trip with a lover was a business trip. As she described it:

"While we were supposed to be reconciling, I discovered he had gone with a woman employee he was attracted to, when someone from the office called to leave a message for him and mentioned the trip. When he returned and I asked him about this, he claimed it was just an ordinary business trip to talk to potential investors in the gallery. But later, he said he didn't tell me about the woman because 'I thought you would be jealous.' After his fourth or fifth story about concealing the trip from me, I saw it as one more example of the way he began to regularly lie to me about almost everything."

Then, when Sandra and Alex began going to a therapist to try to save their marriage, there were still more lies, even though the therapist told them they needed to be honest with each other going forward. Sandra eagerly agreed with this approach, and outwardly Alex acknowledged he agreed also. But he began almost immediately lying to her again to cover up his secrets, which included continuing to see other women. He even tried to cover up his arrest after he was caught soliciting for prostitution, initially claiming he was at a spiritual group meeting, so it was a case of mistaken identity. And later he said the charge was a misunderstanding, because he stopped to talk to a woman on the street because she looked like his mom.

After that, Sandra was more determined than ever to either fix the marriage through therapy or get a divorce. But Alex didn't want to do either, because, Sandra surmised, "I was like an unpaid employee to meet his needs, so he didn't want to get rid of that."

Then, Sandra found Alex trampling on her own boundaries, while insisting that she respect his, which led her to be even more determined to escape what had become a very toxic marriage. It happened when Alex began treating her private journal as something of little importance by tearing out papers in it to use as scratch paper for his financial calculations. Though Sandra asked him to use some other paper, he ignored her, and she felt it was one more show of power.

Finally, after realizing that any chance of saving the marriage was hopeless, since Alex wouldn't change, Sandra was determined to get a divorce, though Alex prolonged the process, because he didn't want her to leave until he found someone else. But again he lied to Sandra to get a better agreement by claiming he hated the business and wanted to go back to accounting. Then Sandra would take a smaller share of the business in the divorce settlement. However, after Alex quickly paid for Sandra's share at a low price, he turned the company into a very successful business and claimed that Sandra never had anything to do with the business. As Sandra observed:

> "So in the end, rather than getting out of the business to become an accountant again, he just used wanting to get out as a ploy to get the business at a lower price. While I created the business and worked with him as an equal partner in the beginning, once he paid me off, he claimed I had nothing to do with the business, though it has been very successful. And now that I am out of his life, he used that success to buy four luxury properties and five expensive cars. He even bought one house as a present for his new wife."

Though it took Sandra several years to finally feel free of what happened, in the end, she was glad to be out of the marriage and Alex's life. The overall experience of dealing with a sociopath and narcissist left her devastated and with a therapist still processing what happened. For her it was like being caught up in a trap from which she couldn't get out. His lies and deceptions helped him manipulate her to get what he wanted, even in the divorce, when he got her to take much less than the business was worth by claiming to be disinterested. He hoped to get her out to soar to even greater heights. She was left with so many regrets, feelings of helplessness, and a loss of confidence in her ability to find someone she could really trust in the future. Yet she needed to get involved in other activities and relationships, even if it hurt at first, to put what happened further into the past in order to move on to a brighter future.

Given Alex's history of lies, Sandra might have done more to check his assessment of the worth of the business to get a better settlement. Or if she just wanted to be out of it, she should try to stop her feelings of regret and loss in order to move on, perhaps with the help of a therapist or support group.

An Entrepreneur Conned Out of His Money and His Wife

In another case, a sociopath in real estate was able to suck in a vulnerable newbie, "Virgil," from Fresno, California, making him turn over his life savings to learn the success secrets of flipping houses for no money down. Virgil not only lost his money but also his wife. When the scam artist ultimately grew tired of her, she returned to Virgil begging for forgiveness, but he no longer wanted her back. For a time after the con, he was even left homeless, lived in his truck, turned to alcohol and drugs, and nearly committed suicide, until a preacher helped him come back from despair, and lent him some money. Thereafter, he was able to turn his life around and achieve success again. But at the time it all happened, he got sucked in by the con artist's artful manipulations, as he had not recognized him for the predator he was.

Initially, Virgil met the scam artist, "Devon," when Devon was giving a real estate seminar on how to make a fortune flipping properties at a hotel in Los Angeles. After the seminar, Devon arranged for one-on-ones with those interested in learning more, and offered to train them as his partner in return for $10,000 or more—the amount varied based on how much he assessed the mark had in cash. The training involved showing newbies how to select properties where they could persuade a motivated seller to forgo a cash down-payment by giving the buyer a loan. Then, after making some improvements, they could resell the house for much more, so they could repay the loan and make a nice profit for each house.

At the time, Virgil thought the plan was a sure-fire way to make a lot of money quickly, when he had little to invest. He had already started acquiring a few lease-option properties and reselling the contract within a few days for only a few hours' work, netting about $2,000 per sale. But he wasn't making enough to leave his full-time job at a convenience store, where he had worked for over a decade.

Then, Virgil saw an ad in a real estate magazine about Devon's seminar in L.A., and he was impressed that Devon had written a book on how he had made millions on lease-option sales by buying them and flipping them. So he drove to the seminar from his home in Virginia, eager to learn more.

At the seminar, held in a large hotel ballroom, he and about three dozen other attendees were quickly impressed by Devon's presentation and the display of his books that contributed to his air of authority. As he appeared on stage in a fashionable black suit and red power tie, he appealed to the audience with the same kind of charm, charisma, and gift of gab characteristic of successful sociopaths. Though not every successful salesman can be characterized as a sociopath, Devon used other techniques characteristic of a sociopath, such as telling extravagant lies and manipulating Virgil and several other participants into putting up money

–sometimes their life savings—to support his grandiose lifestyle based on a foundation of fraud.

For example, after pumping everyone up with the question: "Are you ready to be a real estate millionaire?" he told a mostly made up story about going from rag to riches himself by buying lease-option properties with no money down. Likewise, any one of them could start small and work their way up by getting bigger and bigger deals to build a fortune.

Devon's talk excited Virgil, and after the seminar, he, along with other wannabe real estate entrepreneurs, crowded around Devon to set up their own personal meeting. At their one-on-one, Devon convinced Virgil to join his elite team of property flippers. It was like Devon was putting on the charm of the initial wooing stage to draw Virgil into his web, though the opportunity wasn't real—a key difference between a sociopath presenting a faux business opportunity which he knows is false and a salesman pitching an opportunity that is real and that he believes it is.

Virgil eagerly jumped in, reeled in by Devon's words that made him feel special and chosen to have this special opportunity. But given his blind trust, Virgil missed a key warning sign when Devon asked Virgil how much money he had in cash and on his credit cards. After Virgil told him he had about $20,000, Devon told him that would be enough. But instead of recognizing this request as a way that Devon could figure out how much he could get from him, Virgil saw Devon's invitation as giving him the chance of a lifetime. As Virgil described it:

"Devon said he wanted me to quit my job and move to L.A. to help him grow his seminar and real estate business. He said he would start me at a salary of $75,000 a year, along with a bonus for sales, and I would be earning around $300,000 a year after two years. It sounded like a really great opportunity, though it involved such a big change. So I hesitated, not sure what to do."

At this point, Virgil should have considered Devon's offer more critically, since it involved such a tremendous change that would pull him away from his longtime support network in another city. Moreover, he had just met Devon who was now presenting him with such an attractive offer that it could rationally be viewed as a "too good to be true," that is used to pull the vulnerable into a scam. But Virgil wanted to believe so much—too much—that he ultimately succumbed after some more effective persuasion by Devon.

Devon applied this persuasion after sensing Virgil's hesitation. Devon invited Virgil to think about the offer, and to help convince him, he invited Virgil to bring his wife to Stockton, California, where he was giving another seminar later that month. If he accepted the offer, Devon offered to make him his "Number 2 Guy." It was a classic sales technique of sweetening the pot, and it helped to sway Virgil by giving him time to make the commitment and offering even more. In turn, Virgil returned home, eager to get his wife Darla involved, which proved an even bigger mistake. Though initially she was reluctant to go, she was soon captivated by Devon's charm, too.

A few weeks later, at the seminar, Virgil again saw how Devon charmed the crowd, which had now grown to about 100 attendees, with the same upbeat entrance, hard luck to super success story, and an assurance that all the attendees could realize the same success. Then, after the meeting, Virgil introduced Darla to Devon, and he failed to notice how Devon was already working his charm on Darla. He thought Devon was just showing off his winning personality as with everyone, unaware of the risks ahead.

Thus, when Devon called in the morning to see if they were in or out, Virgil quickly said yes, saying they would need just a few weeks to get the money together by selling their home in Fresno, and he also had to tie up some things at work.

In his enthusiasm for his vision of this new life ahead, Virgil missed the next warning signal: when he asked if they needed an agreement, and Devon said it wasn't necessary. After all, he assured Virgil: "We're now a family. And my word is my bond."

Since Devon sounded so sincere and the image of them being a warm happy successful family was so compelling, Virgil didn't press Devon about the agreement. He was afraid to show any lack of trust, though in reality, his trust was misplaced. He had been lured in by the image which Devon presented to the world, rather than the real person underneath with the soul of a sociopath—eager to win at any cost, with no concern about any-one who could get hurt along the way. He had no conscience, no guilt, and an ability to charm others into believing his misrepresentations and lies.

Over the next few weeks, Devon pulled Virgil even further into his trap. Among other things, he talked to Virgil regularly about their plans to do real estate deals in L.A. and travel around the country setting up seminars on how others could do lease-option "no money down" deals. Meanwhile, Virgil and Darla prepared to move by getting rid of things they didn't need and putting their home up for sale—both to move and to have more money to invest in Devon's real estate deals. It was the perfect set up for making Virgil even more vulnerable, since in trusting Devon, he had given up his house and would turn over most of his money. Yet Devon's charm and persuasiveness convinced him to do this.

So Virgil didn't assess the potential dangers of the risks, he only saw the success side of the equation, so his own misled thinking contributed to Devon taking advantage of him, much like a predator looks for weak-nesses in its prey and selects the most vulnerable to cull from the herd.

Thus, clearly, Virgil should have taken more time to assess the deal and consider the potential downside if things didn't work. He should have gotten involved more slowly in a step by step fashion to see how the first stage worked before moving forward, rather than plunging ahead in what was an all or nothing scheme which made him totally under Virgil's control, since he had moved and invested almost all of his money with Devon.

Virgil also missed the cues that Devon was drawing Darla to him when he talked to her at the end of their phone calls. Rather, Virgil was pleased that Darla now seemed glad they were moving to L.A. Caught up with the details of preparing to move and excited about the potential for success which Devon always spoke about, Virgil didn't realize how Devon was building a relationship with his wife through these calls. He felt secure knowing that Devon was married, so he believed these calls simply reinforced Darla backing his plans to move. But they opened the door to still another betrayal.

Likewise, Virgil thought Devon was fulfilling his end of their partnership of providing new opportunities, the time Devon called excitedly about his new client in Montana, and he asked Virgil to travel there to teach the man and his wife the real estate lease-option business. Making the offer seem even more desirable, Devon offered to pay him $5,000 for the week he would spend there.

So the next day, Virgil got the money to invest in their partnership by maxing out his credit cards to get the $20,000, and he ignored a banker's cautions about what he was doing.

Thus, like a ship captain ignoring any warnings of a squall ahead, he left the bank with all the money from his credit card and only a few thousand left in the bank. But his dreams of getting rich, combined with Devon's slick charm and persuasiveness, helped to convince him that this was the thing to do now. Little did he realize that this trip to Montana was really a way to get him out of the picture for a week, while Devon courted and won over Darla. Though Devon was married, he didn't care about his wife either. Like a true sociopath, he only wanted what was good for him; it didn't matter who else got hurt in the process.

Over the next week, Virgil had no idea anything was wrong, after he flew to Montana and consulted with the clients, a young couple in their mid-thirties. Even though after several days, the couple told Virgil that they had reservations about working with Devon, Virgil was quick to defend Devon, as if to protect his own belief against anyone who would attempt to tear that down. As Virgil explained:

"The couple told me they met with Devon a few times and paid him over $50,000 for his assistance in locating and choosing the best prime properties to make the most profit. But after that, Devon only spoke to them on the phone a few times, so he couldn't give them specific advice about what to do. So they were becoming increasingly skeptical about Devon and his intentions. And they said they spoke to some other couples they met at Devon's seminar who had the same experience.

"But I still wanted to believe. So I told them 'I'm sure Devon means well. He's just so busy, which is why he sent me to help you.'"

So for now, Virgil's comments not only helped to reassure Devon's clients that all was well, but also convinced himself. Wanting to believe, Virgil pushed aside any concerns about Devon's sincerity after the couple shared their experience, and continued consulting with them on how to best judge any properties they might consider buying. In turn, his continued belief was supported by Devon's facade, of a super-successful real estate tycoon with an authoritative book, successful seminar company, and million dollar deals. Virgil never thought to consider that this facade was based on lies.

Devon soon took further advantage of him. The next sign that something was wrong occurred when Virgil arrived back in Fresno and he felt distant from his wife when he tried to kiss her hello in the kitchen. Though she said everything was fine, she told him that Devon had called and wanted Virgil to fly to L.A. to meet him personally. He had something very important to tell him, and Darla didn't know what this was.

So Virgil flew there the next day, and he learned the grim news as he sat across from Devon in the living room of his $3 million L.A. mansion— Darla was leaving him for Devon. As Virgil tells it:

"I was in complete shock and speechless. As if he was casually describing a business deal, he said 'While you were in Montana, I saw your wife in Virginia, and she came here and we got to know each other. So now I'm sleeping with her, and she's moving in with me in L.A.'

"I could hardly believe what he said. It was so unexpected, since I loved Darla so much and thought she felt the same about me. We had been together for nearly twenty years now. So it was a real shock to hear that Darla had decided to move out and move in with someone who we had only met several weeks before."

Yet, that is the charm of a sociopath in initially wooing a victim. Just like Devon had earlier convinced Virgil to put his life savings into a proposed business partnership, now he had pulled Virgil's wife Darla into the web, using Virgil's trip to Montana as a way to get him out of town so he could spend time with her . Yet, rather than walk away, as he should have done at this point to not risk any further loss, or perhaps reach a settlement with Devon for him to go away, Virgil did nothing. Instead, since he had little money left after quitting his job, selling his house, and giving most of his money to Devon, Virgil agreed when Devon said they could still proceed with their business deal. Almost in a detached fugue state, like a robot, Virgil answered: "Okay. I'll still move to L.A. like I planned, so we can be partners and I can learn from you."

So Devon continued to talk about how they could promote his seminars and speaking business, and he told Virgil he could stay with a couple who were his business partners in the area. Then, as Devon went to the kitchen to prepare lunch for them, Virgil sought to mentally justify to himself what had happened and why it made sense to stay. It was the kind of mental processing that many victims go through to find an explanation they can feel comfortable with emotionally. While sociopaths have no emotions, leading them to make cool, confident, rational choices to achieve their ends, victims typically are emotionally devastated by what happens, and if they continue on in the relationship, too weak and afraid to leave, they need some kind of raison d'etre to feel better about why they did what they did.

Soon afterwards, Virgil ignored further signs of Devon's duplicity. For example, after he got to know Devon's business partners who he stayed with for a few days, he learned they had paid Devon over $100,000 for his consulting on buying property, and they felt his advice was too costly and not very good by steering them into deals that didn't work out or they could have simply found on their own.

But still, Virgil went ahead with his arrangement with Devon. The next day, he flew back to Fresno to pack up his things and saw that Darla was already gone, though he later realized she was flying to L.A. to be with Devon while Virgil was flying to Fresno. As Virgil explained in thinking about the situation, "The flights were Devon's way to keep us apart. This way he could make sure that Darla was still committed to join him in L.A. and wouldn't change her mind when she saw me."

Over the next two months, as he sold his house and most of this property, so he could fit everything in a U-Haul to go to L.A., he kept trying to mentally steel himself to seeing Devon and Darla together when he got to L.A., reminding himself that: "Everything will turn out for the best. Even if you can't have your wife anymore, at least you will be Devon's partner and he will help you to become a millionaire."

This mental self-talk was Virgil's way to make sense of what had happened, though he later realized that he should have walked away much sooner. As he explained:

"I should have taken to heart what his former partners had to say about being misled or cheated by him. I should have realized that this showed his lack of character and ethics as a person and businessman."

Of course, there were so many points along the way that should have alerted Virgil that he was dealing with someone not to be trusted. But as they were happening, Virgil didn't recognize that he had been sucked into Devon's web of lies. Only in hindsight did he realize that he was still the naive hopeful, who kept hoping that everything would work out and that anything bad that had happened was simply part of God's plan for him. But he later realized that: "I was opening myself up to be victimized again and again, much like a small kid in school is repeatedly beaten up by the school bully, because he doesn't know how to stand up to the bully for himself."

But at the time Virgil didn't know how to pull himself out of the web; he didn't know how to get off the merry-go-round as it went round and round, creating ever more havoc in his life.

In fact, Devon helped to keep him in the loop by calling him the day after he returned to his nearly empty house in Fresno, his voice sounding much like when he was about to close the sale at a seminar. "I just wanted to check that everything is all a go," he said. "So forget Darla, pack, and move to L.A. so we can go ahead with our partnership, like we planned."

In response, Virgil groggily agreed, since his wife and job were already gone, and he felt he had nothing left to lose. He didn't even get the promised $5,000 for the trip to Montana. While Devon acknowledged the promise, he slipped out of paying with an excuse that kept Virgil on the hook. "Sure, I'll pay you," he agreed. "But my money's tied up in investments, so I don't have enough cash to pay you now. I just have to wait for a few checks to arrive and clear the bank. Then, I can pay you."

It was a classic "delay and don't pay" excuse. But it was convincing enough for Virgil to agree to wait, afraid that otherwise he might completely kill the deal of working with Devon and then never get paid.

Amazingly, what kept Virgil hooked in spite of the loss of his wife, the lies, and excuses is that he still believed that Devon had some kind of secret recipe for him to become a millionaire. And ironically, because he had become so depressed and demeaned by the very situation which Devon had caused him to be in, he felt he needed Devon all the more.

So he continued to remain on board, wanting to believe Devon would finally come through with his money-making secrets and the promised advance. But gradually, Virgil began to observe some cracks in Devon's facade, and that things were not as they seemed. As Virgil described it:

"A few times when I went to some of the clubs in L.A. with Devon, Darla, and the couple I was staying with, I began to notice that Devon was constantly looking about nervously. It was like he was afraid to run into someone he didn't want to see. So I began wondering if Devon was so nervous because if he hadn't paid me, were there others he hadn't paid, too? And if so, how could he afford to live in a $3 million mansion? So I began to think that nothing seemed to add up or be what it seemed."

Yet, even as these suspicions started to come up, Virgil tried to push these concerns away, because he so wanted to believe in the promise of a big opportunity, since he had left behind everything for that. And seeing his wife with Devon made everything even worse. It was like he was coming to realize he was in a house of mirrors, but didn't want to break the glass to see the shattered reality that would be revealed. Instead, Virgil kept thinking, "'It'll work out in the end. God will make everything right."

Thus, for several weeks Virgil tried to maintain the charade by reassuring himself that everything was still fine, though the signs that Devon was really a con artist were everywhere, such as his repeated promises to pay though he never could despite living the high life.

Soon Virgil encountered more and more signs that everything was falling apart, as cracks appeared in Devon's facade. For example, a week after Virgil moved to L.A., Devon asked him to help him buy a Lexus for the company using his credit card so Devon could get a loan, claiming he couldn't buy the car himself, because his ex-wife had ruined his credit. But once he used Virgil's credit card to qualify for the loan, he would make the payments.

So Virgil agreed. But a month later, when Devon didn't make the payments and Virgil still hadn't gotten his money, he had another revelation while talking to Jerry and Judy, Devon's partners who he was staying with, while sitting around their backyard pool. As they talked about the houses they had visited that day, Jerry commented that he and Judy had paid Virgil over $100,000 for his consulting on how to get the best deal, and had to charge their credit cards to pay him. But so far, Jerry and Judy had found that his advice was not very good, since they had been mostly breaking even or netting at most a few thousand on each deal. Devon had advised them to file for bankruptcy after they paid him $100,000 using their credit cards, since they weren't making enough each month to pay back the interest and now their credit was shot. Their situation was much like what he heard from the clients he met with in Montana.

So finally, Virgil had to face reality. When he met with Devon, not only did Devon claim he still couldn't pay him, but told him that he didn't leave the house much anymore, because he was avoiding people who had paid him large sums of money. Soon after that, Virgil discovered that Devon had ended his relationship with Darla and sent her packing. They had had a big fight, after she confronted him about his false promises, such as failing to take her on glamorous trips around the world. She had discovered how little she had left after Devon convinced her to max out her credit card and file for bankruptcy after she had gotten her money. So he had cut off his relationship with her, as sociopaths do when someone confronts them with the truth. Thus she had become a victim along with Virgil.

But though Darla begged Virgil to take her back, he wasn't interested, since he felt betrayed. Even if Devon had manipulated and taken advantage of Darla, he felt it was her choice, and decided it was over between them for good. Then he hung up, feeling devastated. Despite still having feelings for this one-time love of his life, he felt he could never trust her again, since if she committed adultery on him once, she could do it again. Plus he felt bitter about the way she had walked out on him like a greedy opportunist, because of Devon's seductive promises.

Once he faced his shattered reality, Virgil realized that he had to get out of Los Angeles and away from Devon. He called a friend back home in Fresno, explaining that he had been taken in by a rip-off artist and now needed help to get out of L.A. and a place to stay while he got back on his feet.

Once his friend arrived, they left at 6 a.m. As they drove off, he felt finally free of the nightmare that had taken over his life for eight months, starting from when he went to Devon's seminar that had sucked him in. But now, as Virgil commented, "I felt like I was at last speeding out of his trap."

Still, the experience had left him with few resources, so it was a hard way back. Though he at least had a place to stay on his friend's living room couch, he didn't have any money or credit to get a loan. But he was able to pawn Darla's wedding ring, which she had given back to him when she left, for $1,500 . It was enough to buy a used truck, which he slept in for a time, while feeling very lonely and depressed. The victimization by a con-artist sociopath had left him with virtually nothing.

Though Virgil did eventually pull himself back up after finding a real estate sales job, his near destruction at the hands of a sociopath had totally wrecked his life for a while. He had let the charms of a sociopath first draw him in, and for many months after that, he fell victim to Devon's continued promises and manipulations. Even when he began to suspect that things were not as they seemed, he at first denied his suspicions and kept hoping that somehow things would turn around. When they didn't, he stayed, feeling he had nowhere else to go until the very end, when he encountered many other victims who had similarly been beguiled by Devon's charm and promises.

The Wiles of a Sociopath

Thus, much as when a victim lives with a sociopath, a person in a business and personal relationship with a sociopath can go through much the same kind of entrapment process. For in this situation, the sociopath similarly lures a victim into his or her world through an initial charm. Then, he or she lies to artfully manipulate and control with an illusion of continued or future success, and later makes offers, excuses, and explanations to evade any problems that develop. So there is the same initial courtship and honeymoon phase where the sociopath lures the victim into a trap, whether for a personal relationship or business arrangement. Thereafter, as the situation continues, the sociopath gains more and more control by manipulating and exploiting the victim.

But before the final denouement, when the victim comes to sense that things aren't right—such as when Sandra began noticing that Alex was deceiving the artists, and when Virgil discovered that Devon was taking advantage of other "partners" who paid him high sums, while claiming he couldn't pay Virgil, the sociopath at first is able to persuade the victim to remain, via more lies and manipulation. So initially, the victim may want to continue to believe and may be held from breaking away due to other considerations, such as children in Sandra's case, a lack of resources in Virgil's case.

But when the break finally occurs, after escaping from the toxic relationship, the victim is left devastated emotionally and/or financially, and needs to pick up the pieces, such as with the help of a psychiatrist in Sandra's case or by finding a new job, in Virgil's case. Still, at the time, the victim never recognized the sociopath for what he was, not knowing the classic traits and behavior patterns. They simply thought they had been conned by a con-artist.

This lack of recognition is often a problem. So many successful sociopaths are able to continue preying upon many victims because in pursuing their goals of success, they use normally legitimate channels and strategies. Also, they don't normally engage in the kinds of criminal activity that can lead to a jail sentence, such as embezzlement, grand theft, or fraud, when the evidence is clear cut. Or they aren't caught in the more elusive and hard to prove white collar crimes, such as cheating artists of promised funds and cooking the books, like Alex, or using misrepresentation and fraud in complex real estate dealings, like Devon. So the police typically regard their actions as civil wrongs rather than crimes, and the victims are commonly too devastated, lack the funds to pursue any legal action, or the sociopath has no money to collect. So, after the sociopath or victim ends the relationship , the sociopath is free to go on to the next victim and play out a similar pattern or scenario.

Commonly, as in these two cases, where a business relationship is mixed with a personal relationship, the situation can become more complicated and devastating for the victim, since the relationship can continue for many months or years.

By contrast, in business only dealings, the con or sociopathic power plays tend to occur much more quickly, since the sociopath tends to have a more specific short term goal, such as getting more money or a new position, as reflected in the cases described in the next chapter.

CHAPTER 9:
STRICTLY BUSINESS

When you are dealing with a successful sociopath in a strictly or mostly business arrangement, it can be hard to know if the person is actually a sociopath, since not all con artists or business people who play power games are sociopaths. For example, a con artist may be scamming others to support a family he loves, or a boss may be showing off her power, because she feels she has to be aggressive to get ahead in a cut-throat office environment. She may even feel guilty when she throws someone under the bus to save her own job, but does so to survive in a super competitive environment.

Thus, it can help to look at the person's behaviors in a broader context to see if the person has a pattern of behaving in a heartless, guilt-free way that is a sign of the sociopath, rather than this being a behavior in response to a particular situation.

One way to identify a sociopath is to learn if the person's pattern of behavior follows the person from job to job or if multiple victims tell a similar story. Often when victims first are victimized at work, they may feel alone and powerless to do anything. But in today's environment of the Internet and social media, you can check out review and rip-off sites to check to see if someone has been a multiple offender. These sites may provide a way to contact other victims, and you may be able to take some actions together. Also, from time to time, scam artists get caught and are featured in news stories about their arrest. Even if it may not be possible to get back any lost money or receive compensation for time spent working for a sociopath, at least it might be some consolation that the law has finally caught up with a scammer who is getting his or her just deserts.

One of the most notorious examples of predation in business is the Bernie Madoff case. Though Madoff was not identified as a sociopath by the mainstream media, his actions showed all the signs of a successful sociopath with multiple victims writ large. In fact, at the time that Madoff was exposed, a number of articles asked that very question: "Is Bernie Madoff a sociopath?" and the general consensus was that he exhibited many of the classic traits, though there was no way to make an official psychological diagnosis.

For example, in a *Salon* article, "Is Bernie Madoff a Sociopath?"[130] Peter Finocchiaro describes how Madoff spoke to New York reporter Steve Fishman in twelve phone conversations, in which he expressed regret for his crimes, claiming it was an accident that spiraled out of control, and bothered him for years. He insisted that despite what he did, he is a good person and not a sociopath. But many of his victims considered him a sociopathic monster, and even if a sociopath expresses remorse, that might not be real; it could all be an act.

Although Finocchiaro can't conclude for certain, even after talking to a clinical professor of psychiatry, if Madoff is a sociopath—since a psychiatrist can't diagnose someone he hasn't interviewed himself—Madoff shows many of the classic traits. For example, on the surface, Madoff was certainly charming, and he readily took the money of many of the victims who had once been friends, and many victims judged him as a conartist with no scruples or conscience. As one of his victims stated in a *CNNMoney* interview: "The man is a monster, a liar, a thief with absolutely no morals, no regrets, no shame." [131] But someone might act that way only in their business dealings, since Finocchiaro suggests there is a spectrum in which some people may appear to have no conscience in their business dealings, but they can be caring about others within a small circle of people they care about, so they can compartmentalize, while some people have no conscience at all.[132]

Mona Ackerman, a clinical psychologist, came to a similar conclusion in "The Psychology Behind Bernie Madoff."[133] As she points out, Madoff did show some responsibility and guilt towards his family, so he was not completely detached from all people, as sociopaths commonly are. Thus, she concludes that Madoff did have sociopathic tendencies that were nurtured in an environment of great social and economic uncertainty after 9/11, where people were seeking a sure thing and fast money return. As Ackerman observes:

"Madoff personified certainty. He gave a lot of people, charities, and bankers the answers they needed.

---

[130] Peter Finocchiaro, "Is Bernie Madoff a Sociopath?" *Salon*, http://www.salon.com/2011/03/02/is_bernie_madoff_a_socipath.

[131] Aaron Smith, "Madoff Mess: Madoff Victims Fire Back: 'The Man is a Monster,'" *CNNMoney*, http://money.cnn.com/2011/02/28/news/companies/madoff_victims

[132] Ibid.

[133] Mona Ackerman, "The Psychology Behind Bernie Madoff," Huffington Post, 1/18/209, http://www.huffingtonpost.com/mona-ackerman/the-psychology-behind-ber_b_151966.html

"At the same time, his clients were getting what they needed. They got rewards and security. . . . For that, they looked away. They ignored warning signs—those remarkable earnings. But when the curtain was pulled back, there was Bernard Madoff, a sociopath—and the till was empty."[134]

And while Madoff did claim remorse for the many victims who suffered major financial losses when his investment scheme collapsed, many felt any of his expression of remorse was just for show to preserve his reputation, which is exactly what a sociopath does. For example, in responding to the question: "Is Bernie Madoff a Sociopath?" on the Neurological Correlates format, a participant calling himself "Swivelchair" pointed out that Madoff's attempts to claim he was a good person and show remorse were simply ploys to redeem his reputation after destroying those around him through their financial ruin.

Likewise, as shown in numerous news stories, he engaged, instead, in numerous actions that are characteristic of a sociopath, such as the following tactics:

1. He used a charm offense by showing he was a successful market maker.
2. He made a play for sympathy, in acknowledging that what he did was "my bad" due to his weakness for drugs, alcohol, and ego.
3. He minimized what he did, by claiming he wasn't as bad as others in history, such as Hitler, and he blamed others in the financial industry for being worse.
4. He rationalized his actions by finding blame elsewhere, such as claiming he had to do it because his customers were greedy.
5. He sought to trivialize the victims' harm, by claiming his victims were exaggerating their financial loss.[135]

While these strictly business encounters with sociopaths may not lead to the same intense emotional devastation that victims commonly feel after a long-term personal relationship with a sociopath, they can certainly result in emotional upheaval and extensive financial losses. They may also undermine a victim's trust in future business dealings based on a fear this might happen again. And victims may feel a great loss of confidence and self-esteem, because of their misjudgment and economic loss.

[134] Ibid.
[135] Swivelchair, ibid.

The following stories illustrate the different ways in which socio-paths—or individuals considered to be sociopaths—can take advantage in business and work settings.

A Film Producer Who Raised Money Through a Boiler Room Operation

When I lived in L.A. for two years seeking to get into the film industry, I met a number of people who in retrospect seemed to qualify as sociopaths, besides my experience with the woman film producer who worked on my film and tried to steal it, that I described earlier. Like her they all had that strong drive to get ahead, and presented themselves as something they were not, such as calling themselves producers and directors, when they had never yet produced or directed anything.

In certain industries, such as the film industry, finance industry, politics, and any position involving sales, the emphasis on attaining material wealth, power, and success seems to have a special appeal for sociopaths. By con-trast, the sociopaths might be less likely to be in other fields which attract individuals who are caring and concerned about others, such as the health professions and human resources. The film industry seems particularly prone to this attraction, since the field is bottom-line oriented, with an emphasis on big box office success, and people use the image of success as a kind of calling card to help open doors for them. Moreover, the stars in the field are actors, who make a living through pretending to be something they are not.

It is in this context that I met another film producer I'll call Victor after a mailing to producers about some of my film projects through my business connecting writers to publishers, agents, and the film industry. I later introduced him to a hopeful writer and cinematographer, Eric, who became one of his true victims, after he spent several weeks reviewing scripts for Victor and never getting paid. And there were hundreds of other victims who invested in his company based on misrepresentations and lost their money, before Victor ended up in jail. He, along with seventeen oth-ers, was charged with running a boiler room sales operation which raised about $25 million for a film, but they only put about $5 million into the film, didn't release other films, and put most of the money into travel and expensive homes and cars.

One of the warning signs that I didn't recognize at the time was Victor's exaggerated claims to have high power connections in Hollywood, such as a brother-in-law who was a well-known film producer, although he had been divorced from his former brother-in-law's sister for several years, so he really no longer had a good connection. Victor also spoke grandly about many of the films his company was producing and how he would like to produce one of mine, once his foreign funding came through to keep me involved, though the funds never did arrive, and he and his associates spent most of the funds from investors on living a lavish lifestyle.

But since I wasn't aware of all this at the time and I was drawn in by Victor's confident talk about film opportunities, I introduced Eric to him, since Eric lived in L.A. and was eager to get into the film business as a writer and cinematographer. So far, he had worked on a number of low-paid jobs on indie film crews as the second camera, and he worked for a volunteer organization providing low-cost script coverage to new screenwriters. When Victor offered him an opportunity reviewing and critiquing scripts for pay, Eric jumped at the opportunity, and he reviewed several hundred scripts for Victor. But Victor never paid Eric anything. Instead, he kept assuring Eric that he would be paid once the foreign funding from China came through. But after three years of being led on by Victor's promises of great opportunities, Eric racked up a bill of nearly $60,000 from reviewing scripts, writing reports, making recommendations, and rewriting some scripts, on which he was promised film credits.

Because of these promises of future rewards, Eric ignored many of the warning signs, such as the cavalier manner in which Victor treated him. For example, several times Eric made appointments to meet Victor at his office, but when Eric arrived, after an hour of freeway driving, Victor wasn't there, and Victor never called or emailed him to say he would be away, even later, after Eric called back several times, Victor finally answered and gave him a perfunctory apology, showing he had little concern about Eric's difficulties. Yet, since Victor kept promising to produce several films on which Eric could participate, Eric pushed aside any concerns about missed meetings and insincere apologies to continue reviewing film scripts for Victor. And despite the continually delayed payments, Eric kept working for Victor, believing Victor's claim that the company would provide a big opportunity once the Chinese funding arrived.

But what Eric didn't know is that the company facade was all show, and there was no foreign investment coming from China or anywhere else. Instead, the claim of big investors was just part of the facade which Victor presented to everyone, just like he bragged about having big studio connections through his brother-in-law, when any such connection had died when he got divorced.

Finally, in mid-2011, reality hit in the form of a federal investigation into a telemarketing boiler room operation that raised over $25 million for two films from over 500 victim-investors, but only produced one for $5 million and used the extra funds for beautiful homes, cars, and foreign travel. Eventually, according to Eric who followed the case, Victor pled guilty as did most of the others, and he was sentenced to four years in prison. So that ended Eric's hopes of collecting the $60,000 payment due for his work or his potentially working on future film projects for Victor. At the same time, the conviction ended Victor's false front as a big-time Hollywood producer.

In this case, Eric should have never followed along so complacently for over three years. Rather than being strung along with a promise to pay once a claimed investment arrived, Eric should have stopped early on, say once his billing was about $2,000 to $3,000, and he should have asked for pay to do any more. Plus, Eric could have done some online research to verify some victims' claims by entering a few key words, and if there were any gaps or discrepancies, he could have dropped out early on, before spending so much time without getting paid.

Likewise, you should be cautious when you face repeated delays and excuses about payments, and you hear that the person has certain high-level connections. If so, you can check out these claims online, and if you discover a pattern of lies, it's time to cut your losses as best you can and move on.

A Publisher on a Rampage Against Any Critiques

Another case of a likely sociopath in business is a small independent publisher who goes on an anger-fueled rampage to destroy anyone who dares to criticize his press.

In this case, one writer, David, sent a proposed project to the editor of this company I'll call the ABC Press, about a book on exposing scams, and publisher, expressed interest and offer a $10,000 advance. But then the publisher "Tom Thompson," wanted to change the book's focus from interviewing several dozen people who experienced different types of scams to writing about a particular scam in which writers, librarians, and others joined together to ruin the reputation of a publishing company, using his own company as an example. Though David wasn't sure he wanted to change the focus of the book or that the effort to expose a publisher who wronged them was a scam, the $10,000 advance seemed tempting. Plus, David had no offers from other publishers, so he felt like this might be his only opportunity for publication.

Yet, even if he currently had no other offers, David should have said no from the get go, because maybe the group claiming the publisher had wronged them could be right. He should have given more weight and credence to his own suspicions. But David was swayed by Thompson's seemingly mild-mannered appearance and offer to pay half of the $10,000 up front. So he agreed to Thompson's offer, making him vulnerable to being conned himself.

Then, as if the con was now being launched, things got weird. First, the publisher wanted to fly out to meet with David at his home in Portland to discuss what to say in the book, which was unusual, since normally publishers do not meet with authors, much less fly across the country to meet them. Normally, they do almost everything via phone calls, letters, and emails, and commonly assistants or editors handle these tasks, in fact. Also, it was unusual that the publisher said he would bring half the advance, a check for $5,000, to their meeting.

Complicating the arrangements further, Thompson asked David to edit a book from another writer, and David proposed to do so at his usual hourly rate, with a cap of only $800 for the full manuscript, since Thompson said he just wanted to fix the obvious mistakes like misspellings and bad grammar, so the writer wouldn't be embarrassed by such errors. But after getting the manuscript, David discovered so many errors that he felt more extensive rewriting was necessary, and he couldn't properly revise the full manuscript on the publisher's budget. Or did the publisher really only want a cursory edit, which would result in an unprofessional manuscript?

To make sure, David sent what he revised in a half-hour, and since the publisher was out of town, his executive editor gave him the go-ahead to do more. So David sent in another hour of edits the following day, to which the editor gave another go ahead, and after another hour of editing, he sent a $300 bill for his hours thus far. But after Thompson returned from his trip, everything turned even weirder. A few days later, the editor wrote to him saying that the publisher's experience with David in handling the editing job made him unwilling to continue any relationship. So he wouldn't come to Portland and was withdrawing his offer to publish David's manuscript. And when David asked about his payment for editing after he got three requests from the editor to do more, the editor sent a letter saying that Thompson had decided not to pay him since he didn't finish the book. When David tried to contact Thompson to discuss things, Thompson wouldn't return his phone calls or emails.

But even more chilling was a letter he received a few days after his last email. In the letter, Thompson now blamed him for all kinds of unspecified losses in response to his billing for $300 payment. It was like the kind of "blame the victim" response given by a sociopath should a victim dare to question anything the sociopath is doing. As the letter threatened:

> "When a plumber undertakes to repair your bathroom for an agreed amount, and after spending two hours on the job, then tells you that it is going to cost far more than agreed, you do not pay the plumber, you sue him for fraud.
>
> "Your professional misbehavior has caused us and our author economic loss because you failed to complete the job you agreed to do for a specific amount of money that was agreed. We suggest you write the matter off or we will sue you for the enormous damages you have done to us."

David was stunned. What enormous damages could Thompson possibly be talking about, since David spent only 2½ hours editing a manuscript which needed a more comprehensive edit than he originally expected? Thompson could easily find someone else to do the job; there was no damage to the manuscript or anything else; and editing is not like a plumbing job where a plumber might break pipes or cause water damage due to errors on the job. And the threat to sue him for enormous but unspecified damages over a $300 bill seemed absurd, like bringing out a cannon to swat down a fly.

Under the circumstances, David did exactly the right thing. He dropped any further pursuit of his money or any further contact with the publisher, much as one should do when confronted by an irrational driver in a road rage incident. It's a no-win situation with a person determined to win. Though the letter could be an idle threat to keep David from pursuing the matter, it could also be the beginning of an unpleasant escalation from someone out of revenge and ready and willing to attack, especially when David discovered that Thompson had a history of suing writers, librarians, libraries, and universities for millions in response to expressions of opinion and decisions not to buy his books.

David discovered the publisher's litigation history when he decided to check out the publisher after getting that strange, vindictive letter. That's when he discovered that the publisher had a reputation as a vanity publisher posing as a traditional publisher, so its catalog included a few books it published alongside most of its books which were paid for by the writers. But worse, the media reported that the ABC Press used a false defamation lawsuit to silence a critic who characterized Thompson's books as being of poor quality and not worth the high cost. In the lawsuit, ABC asked for $4 million in damages, and sued not only the writer who had posted the comments, but the school he worked for, and at one time, the suit included a librarian and library.

The suit was an example of legal bullying, and the company made further threats against a blogger who posted two blogs about the company's previous legal actions. In response, many individuals and writers' organizations had come to the support of the writer who was sued on the grounds that freedom of speech includes the freedom to criticize and this publishing company should not use the courts to silence and intimidate its critics. Ironically, as David realized, the book that Thompson wanted him to write by adapting his book on scams was a book to attack any writers and organizations that supported the writer he sued by claiming they were scam artists who wanted to extort money from him. So Thompson wanted David to write the book to discredit these individuals and organizations, get them to stop supporting the writer and organizations he sued, or even set the stage for a suit against them, too.

With some more digging online, David discovered even more negative information about Mr. Thompson, which included getting into a power struggle with his students when he was a professor at a small college because he thought they were moving their desks too slowly into a circle. So he not only began yelling angrily at the students, but fired his teaching assistant for urging him to calm down. Eventually, the incident led to the college dean offering Thompson early retirement, but instead he negotiated a medical leave to go to a special rehabilitation program, claiming a heart condition and depression. After two weeks, he left the program, claiming his doctor ordered a relaxing vacation to help him recover, but instead he went on a world tour for several months, and when the college learned about his trip and sought to terminate him from the school, he refused to resign since he was a tenured professor, which led to a two-week public trial, which the college finally won, though it cost nearly $500,000. It won by showing Thompson was terminated for gross academic misconduct, abusing his medical leave, and taking time from his academic duties to spend time working on his press that had become a business earning millions each year.

For David, these discoveries helped him feel relieved the publisher had turned him down, and he felt better about ending a relationship with a publisher with questionable business practices. The $300 he lost was a small price to pay for this result. And soon afterwards, he found a traditional publisher that offered a small advance and he got his book published.

So in the end, David did exactly the right thing in ending the relationship, and his research helped him better understand what happened and feel better about the end result. He realized the publisher was very likely a sociopath—or at least had the major behaviors of one, and he was glad to have escaped being drawn into what seemed like a questionable, self-serving book to write.At the time it happened, David thought of the contract collapse and non-payment as the result of a business deal gone south. He didn't realize that he was dealing with a publisher who showed all the signs of being a sociopath, starting with wooing him with a very promising contract and manipulating him to change his book to get back at the writers and organizations who supported the other writers and institutions he sued for millions for having a negative opinion about him and his company. Plus Thompson immediately cut David as soon as he pointed out problems with the book, blamed David for fraud when he pointed out that the manuscript had more problems than expected, and threatened to sue David for far more than the small $300 amount he was asking for payment. At least when David decided not to pursue his $300 claim, he didn't have to worry about becoming another victim of Thompson's anger and lawsuits. He could move on without being further caught in a trap.

A Marketing Promoter Who Promised a Lot and Ripped People Off

Sociopaths can also conceal their true character in the business world behind a facade of strong family relationships, whether they have actual feelings for family members or not, because of the ability many of them have to compartmentalize. So they might behave as a sociopath in the business world, where they act without a conscience and lie repeatedly to manipulate victims, but they may be totally different with their family, when business isn't involved. Classically, psychiatrists and psychologists have considered sociopaths to have the characteristic personality traits and behaviors in all aspects of their life, but this appears to not to be the case. For example, in the Madoff case, some psychologists felt he had the ability to compartmentalize, so he could without conscience rip off billions from victims in pursuing his international Ponzi scheme, while feeling some responsibility and concern for the effect of his actions on his family.

That's what Emily, a media consultant, found when Shirley, a workshop organizer and events planner, hired her and made expansive promises. When they first met, Emily had been doing PR for one of one of Shirley's sisters, Beth, who was promoting her new boutique, and Emily came to the ribbon cutting ceremony. At once Shirley praised Emily for her great work for Beth, indicated she owned several businesses, and could use Emily's help in developing some books on financial planning for her. In fact, Shirley told Emily she would have plenty of work for her, because she had so many clients who needed help with PR, and she expected many more.

So initially, all seemed fine. Emily was impressed with Shirley's style and air of self-assurance, and Shirley's connections with a dozen family members at the store opening made her seem even more warm-hearted and credible. Thus, Emily overlooked what might have been the first warning sign that Shirley wasn't completely on the up-and-up: Shirley wanted her to rewrite an already written manual on "Planning Your Financial Future" that she used in her workshops, because it was written by someone else. But now Shirley wanted to do these workshops on her own and needed her own book to sell there. However, she couldn't just take his book and put her name on it, which would infringe on his copyright. So as Shirley told Emily:

"I want you to update it by changing the wording enough, so there's no plagiarism. As long as you can rewrite it so the copy is different, I can make it my own."

At this point, Emily should have said no, since the enterprise was dubious. But she agreed, despite her initial concerns about the legality and ethics of the project, given Shirley's appearance as a very successful and self-assured workshop leader. Although Emily usually worked on a retainer or pay-as-you-go credit card arrangement, she agreed when Shirley asked her to take a check as a down payment and assured her that she could pay the rest that weekend at a big "Start Up the Right Way" conference she was sponsoring with another entrepreneur. She even invited Emily to be one of the presenters to talk about her business, and maybe she could get some clients from the conference. Thus, Emily spent the next three days rushing to finish as much of Shirley's 150 page book as she could, and was able to do half. She emailed Shirley a copy a day before the conference, and brought some additional edited pages when she arrived to speak to the group.

But as it turned out, the conference was a total bust. Instead of a promised turnout of 100 participants, only thirty-five attended, and Emily wasn't able to speak. She was only given time to make a one- minute announcement at the end of conference to about twenty people who were still there. Worse, Shirley said she couldn't pay the balance because she and her partner lost money on the conference and still had hotel bills to pay. Then, she put all the blame on her partner for going ahead with the conference, even though the prepaid attendance was much lower than expected. So now, despite the ritzy surroundings of an A-list hotel, Shirley pled poverty and hoped Emily would understand why she couldn't pay her all she owed her. Plus, she told Emily that she would be getting outstanding checks soon and that she expected a half a dozen new projects to come through.

Lulled by Shirley's reassurances and trying to be understanding and sympathetic, Emily agreed. But three days later Shirley's check bounced, though she blamed a bank snafu and promised to get everything straightened out the next day. However, Shirley now came up with a series of other excuses of why she couldn't pay, though she made two small payments of $100 and $50 a month apart, as if to placate Emily with some token payments.

But, over the next six weeks, the mixture of promises of great opportunities combined with excuses for not paying continued. For example, Shirley said she was flying to L.A. to work out some deals with her PR associate and they were having a free seminar to attract clients for several thousand dollar packages, but that event only sold one package, so there was no money to pay Emily. And Shirley reported that several other deals for PR clients fell through. What especially disturbed Emily, though, was that Shirley was continuing to give her reasons why she couldn't pay.

Certainly, many business problems might occur for anyone in business, not just a sociopath. Companies run into cash flow and payment problems all the time. But what should have made Emily become suspicious early on was the use of promises and lies to avoid paying her, as well as Shirley's attempt to shift blame to Emily when she claimed that the project was only half finished, so she couldn't sell it to make money from this to pay Emily, although Emily had divided the book into two halves that could be sold separately. She also lied by claiming she had offered Emily an ad in a magazine she published, though she had not made such an offer and the magazine was not published, nor was she the publisher. Plus she spoke about her need to pay the rent for a part-time office in an elegant building, so she looked like she owned a very successful company. Yet, while she could pay that, she couldn't find enough to pay Shirley even though she asked her to continue working on the book while floating tantalizing promises of work to come.

Probably in this situation, Emily's best response was to pull out of the project and cut her losses, since the amount in question was not enough to take Shirley to court. Yet ever hopeful, Emily remained ready to continue working on the book, though she pursued the best strategy of waiting to get more money before doing anything more.

Finally, matters came to a head because the excuse that bothered Emily the most was Shirley's statement that she would be going out of town for ten days on a cruise with her family, so she couldn't pay anything more until she got back. In Emily's view, she had tried to be understanding and patient; but now it seemed like Shirley was going to keep giving her new excuses to delay paying her anything, and after Emily sent Shirley a notice saying she would start adding 10 percent interest to the unpaid balance, Shirley now claimed she didn't owe the full amount based on Emily's hourly rate, since Emily had only completed half of the book—a claim she had never made before.

As a result, Emily was furious. She felt like she was being played, with non-payment combined with future promises and reasons for not paying in the present. Why couldn't Shirley pay if she could afford vacation travel and a luxury office suite? Shirley's promises and excuses for repeated payment delays didn't make sense, although in hindsight, her actions reflect the behavior pattern of a sociopath, such as her attempt to blame Emily, the continued effort to manipulate Emily to continue to work on the book with false promises, and the effort to maintain a false front to impress others.

But feeling anything she did was a losing battle, eventually, Emily decided to make the best agreement under the circumstances. She said she would accept Shirley's claim that she owed half if Shirley would pay her now and agree to not expect any more work from her in the future, and Shirley did pay that. Afterwards, disillusioned by what happened and feeling like she had been played, Emily began to check online into Shirley's claims about her many successful businesses, and she soon discovered she was far from the only one who had been taken in by Shirley's promises and lies. For example, she found a series of scathing reports on Yelp that described Emily's financial business, which I'll call The Finance Wizard. Among them were these:

"TFW does not do what it promises. They took fees from my clients, but no service was provided."

"I understand that Shirley might have ended her business as TFW and that is a good thing. She took thousands of dollars from me and did not provide me with usable financial advice and led me into bad investments. In fact, she lied multiple times and never contacted any businesses on my behalf to help me raise money. Stay away from her and any business connected with her name. She will rip you off."

"Well at last the BBB has scored Shirley Armstrong and her bogus company a F!...If anyone comes across this review and has been screwed over by Shirley, let's get together and turn this thief in."

After reading such statements, Emily realized she was not alone, and that Shirley had been manipulating her with promises, lies, and excuses, using the lure of claimed big opportunities that never came through as a way to get her to do what she wanted in revising the book. But then she sought ways to get out of paying, including a promise to pay sometime in the future, accompanied by a reason why she couldn't pay now. Though Emily didn't realize Shirley was engaging in a common pattern of sociopathic behavior in business, that's what Shirley was doing—and since she had been blasted for such behavior with others, this was evidence that her actions with Emily was no mere fluke. She had a pattern of victimizing many others, avoiding a penalty for her actions, and moving on to the next, after she no longer needed the money or involvement of the person she left behind. At least, Emily was able to work out a compromise to get paid half of what was due by finally confronting Shirley and ending the relationship.

Working for a Boss Who Acts Like a Sociopath

Besides being a victim of a sociopath who takes advantage of customers, clients, and service providers, another common situation is working for a boss who treats an employee with little care or concern and may revel in power games, whereby the boss enjoys manipulating an employee. However, a boss may not have to use the charm that often is the first stage of luring in the victim, unless the boss is doing the hiring and presents the company as a great place to work. In many cases, though, such a charm appeal is not necessary, because the prospective employee is eager for the job or has been hired by a company owner or HR manager, who assigns that employee to the boss. So often the employee victim is already on the job when the manipulation and abuse starts.

Still, the boss may use this charm offensive in other ways, such as on higher-ups and other managers and supervisors, who continue to regard the boss highly, even as he or she is mistreating the employees he or she manages. As long as the results are good, as long as the workers are productive, that is commonly what counts to the higher-ups. Thus, as long as the employees are doing their job, a sociopathic boss can get away with his or her behavior. Sometimes this behavior can so terrorize the employees and undermine their confidence that they remain on the job, afraid to leave given the difficulties of finding another job or getting a good recommendation, if they stand up to a boss who has the power.

The following stories illustrate examples of bosses behaving badly, drawn from interviews I conducted with several dozen employees and employers for the book: *A Survival Guide for Working with Bad Bosses.*[136] At the time, I never thought to consider the bosses as sociopaths; I and the interviewees simply called them bad bosses, primarily because they exercised their power over their employees in an abusive, exploitive way, and sometimes they seemed to play power games to show how far they could go in controlling their employees to do what they wanted. While these are characteristic behaviors of a sociopath, the term was generally not used to describe behavior of people who were successful in the workplace.

A Wolf in Sheep's Clothing

In some cases, a boss who does the hiring can entice a prospective employee into what becomes a terrible, soul-crunching environment, much like a wolf can entice a sheep into his lair. That's what Shauna experienced when she began her first year of teaching in an elementary school on a small Indian reservation on the prairies. The principal, Dr. Ryan, used his charm, as successful sociopaths do, to lure Shauna into accepting the job. When she experienced his day-to-day actions, which included humiliating the students and using school resources for his personal benefit, such as driving the school van instead of his car for personal use, she felt she could do little. She had already been caught in his trap and had to work there for at least a year. Initially, she had been drawn to the school though the salary was lower than the nearby public school jobs, because she was inspired by the charm of the principal, Dr. Ryan, when she met him at a school jobs fair and he explained his philosophy of helping to educate the underprivileged. She felt a few years of teaching in this challenging environment would also help her find a good teaching job in the local public school system.

But soon, Shauna, like many other teachers, began to feel that Dr. Ryan's words were all a sham, such as when he told the fourth grade students they would probably end up in jail or as drunken bums in the gutter,

---

[136] Gini Graham Scott, *A Survival Guide for Working with Bad Bosses*, New York: AMACOM, 2006.

and told other elementary school students that they would "amount to nothing better than 'rez dogs.'" While Dr. Ryan had a great charm when he talked to the public, he didn't follow through in getting funds or community support for school programs, and he didn't attend the cultural events held at the school, such as round dances and feasts.

Worse, some of his actions bordered on criminal, such as using school property and funds for personal use, and using the school van instead of his car to drive a sixty mile round trip commute from his home to work each day. He routinely delegated numerous administrative tasks to first-year teachers and took many days off during the entire year, including spending a day on the golf course on the students' last day of school.

Dr. Ryan also regularly bullied and harassed the teachers and was especially abusive to one young teacher he asked out, though he was living with another woman. After she refused him, he frequently yelled at her and reduced her to tears. Additionally, Dr. Ryan pried into the teachers' private lives and asked them personal questions about their families, children, and romantic lives. He spoke about other staff members negatively behind their backs, and used the teacher evaluations like a club to insure conformity with his orders and discourage teachers from resisting or complaining, telling them such actions would negatively affect their evaluation.

When Shauna sought to discuss some of her concerns, she faced repeated retaliation from Dr. Ryan for the remainder of the school year. For example, he falsely reported her poor performance to other teachers and to the principals of other districts, where she was applying for a job for the next year, although she had previously received a glowing evaluation. This was his way of getting revenge, since Shauna had dared to resist him.[137]

In short, Dr. Ryan was a "nightmare boss," who had all the trappings of being a sociopath, from being charming when he wanted to be, to treating the teachers like his personal chattel, who he variously humiliated, insulted, and blamed as a matter of course. Plus he took advantage of the system to do what he wanted, such as using a van like a personal car and taking an extra day to play golf, which delayed the start of the school year. Given the power differential, there was little that Shauna could do that first year except grin and bear it, since any resistance or even an attempt to discuss the problem would lead to retaliation again her, just as Dr. Ryan retaliated against any teacher who resisted him in any way. At least the young teacher who had refused his advances found a job in another county the following year, so she could escape his clutches—usually the best way of dealing with a sociopathic boss who has power over you.

---

[137] Scott, pp. 84-86.

So what should Shauna have done? Unfortunately, given the power differential, she wasn't in a good position to do anything overtly, and being a whistleblower to a higher administrator might have quickly ended her career, although she could look for any opportunity to join any kind of investigation initiated by someone else. Then, too, Shauna might have talked to the other teachers, after she saw them humiliated or taken advantage of in some way. Maybe if enough teachers joined together, they could collectively complain to Dr. Ryan's superiors, and then maybe could be taken seriously.

If you are in a lower power position with a sociopathic boss, probably the best options are to leave if you can, wait it out for the opportunity to do something where you don't damage your own career prospects, or see if you can join forces with enough others in a similar position to effect change.

In another case, Julie had a sociopathic boss who actually engaged in criminal activities. He first invented a cover story about being the boss of a network of travel agencies with private jets and claimed he had come from the East Coast, where this travel empire was based, to start a new branch in the San Francisco Bay Area, which is where Julie met him. Then, he used his charm to create a company with a dozen travel escorts recruited from a *San Francisco Chronicle* ad to lead trips, and he engaged the help of a local singles magazine publisher to help him promote his trips to singles. Even large restaurants and galleries jumped on board his seemingly successful travel juggernaut which had increasingly large singles parties in trendy restaurants and clubs, until after he wrote a half-dozen bad checks the night of a gala singles party that was designed to shore up his whole fantasy empire and the whole edifice crashed down. But when not enough people turned up, so that he didn't have enough money to cover the bad checks, he skipped town. Later, he was captured and arrested in San Diego, when a police officer stopped him for making an illegal left turn and discovered warrants out for his arrest.

Although no one called him a sociopath at the time, his actions were those of a sociopath who built his alcohol-fueled fantasies of great wealth and success into a story that sucked in multiple victims, many of whom lost money or contributed hundreds hours of unpaid work into a sociopathic dream that turned into a nightmare.

Here's how I described his rise and fall, adapted from my account in *A Survival Guide for Working with Bad Bosses*:

> It all began after the travel company head, Rex, put an ad in the *San Francisco Chronicle* for tour escorts . . . Soon, Rex had a dozen or so escorts on tap for the tours, a new vice president of travel sales, and a blonde, twenty-something secretary who looked like a model. He set

up a trendy-looking corporate office suite with a half dozen rooms, including a board room with a long table for meetings.

But the meetings were mostly devoted to dreamy discussions about the great trips that the company hoped to set up. But after several months, none of the customers had actually gone on one of these trips.

Meanwhile, Rex used his charm to persuade vendors to give him credit, promising to pay as soon as expected funds from headquarters came through. But despite tantalizing flyers for glamorous trips to exotic locations, not enough people signed up for any of the trips to take place, though Rex kept taking in deposits and telling clients they would be on the next trip.

Soon there were increasing signs of money problems, and Rex moved the company account from bank to bank. Though he had trouble making the payroll each week, he acted like nothing was wrong, relying on his usual debonair charm that was so persuasive with everyone.

Yet, despite these signs of financial difficulties, the promotional parties continued with local business executives and young singles, and Rex played the genial host. Part of the problem is that he preferred the aura of local celebrity to the day-to-day responsibilities of running a business. Meanwhile, people continued to be captivated by Rex, and no one working for the company seemed to want to acknowledge there could be a problem and risk upsetting the fun rounds of parties and aura of glamour that Rex exuded.[138]

Unfortunately, as Rex's story illustrates, individuals who encounter a likely sociopath in a position of power can be so swayed by the person's charm or the glamour of his position and schemes that they are unaware there could be a problem. Or they don't have the power to do anything, since their boss or leader is in charge, so they go along to get along. If anyone speaks up, they are likely to get fired, so the only real options are to talk individually with co-workers in a similar situation to possibly take some actions as a group, or quit.

The ax finally fell at a gala singles event Rex organized, expecting that the cover charges would pay for the cost of the party and then enough people would sign up for the trips so he could cover other expenses and debts for the past three months. Unfortunately, the event was poorly attended and the receipts came nowhere near meeting the outstanding bills to pay

[138] Ibid., pp. 161-162.

for it. As a result, the next day Rex fled his small apartment, leaving in his wake several bounced checks to the hotel, musicians, and caterer, whom he had charmed into accepting a check for payment in full the night of the party, rather than getting the usual deposit.

Then, after Rex was stopped in Southern California for making an illegal left turn, his long past as a poseur came to light. When the police did a warrants check, they discovered he was wanted up north, and they found a stolen credit card machine in his car; presumably so he could finance a new start in Southern California. He was charged with grand theft for more than $14,000 in bounced checks that final night, though there was about $50,000 in other outstanding payments to employees and other creditors, since we all had been dupes suckered in by Rex's charm.[139] However, there was never any mention of sociopathy at the time; everyone simply thought of Rex as a con man who had cheated them, when, in fact, Rex had taken all of us for a kind of sociopathic ride. With the characteristic charm of a sociopath, he beguiled everyone with his stories of running a huge travel empire, and perhaps Rex came to believe much of the story himself, due to the drugs and alcohol from the frequent parties he put on or attended to pursue his dreams of success in singles travel. So dozens of people eagerly signed up to participate as travel hosts and contributors, but nobody checked out the reality of his story or wondered why this seemingly successful travel company CEO was living with almost no furniture and a sleeping bag in a one-room apart in a seedy part of the city. Everyone simply accepted him for what he claimed to be, based on his false mask.

Then, conscience-free, he convinced a number of unwitting banks and vendors to help him continue his scheme, until it ultimately collapsed, as schemes based on falsehoods often do. His gala party was supposed to be his crowning success, even though not one person who paid had actually gone on a trip. But until that fateful night, his continuing and expanding web of lies had helped him to keep his massive fraud going until its collapse.

Obviously, what all the people who became victims of his fraud—from the employees to the vendors—should have done is check out his story. Everyone, including me, should have asked more questions and asked for more details about his past trips when he was back East. We all should have become suspicious more quickly, when there were payment delays, and the employees might have been more suspicious seeing signs of problems, such as Rex's frequent hangovers, and repeated meetings with bankers to open new accounts as the company's financial affairs grew more desperate.

---

[139] Scott, p. 162.

By the same token, if you begin to see signs of a cover-up in a business, do more checking on the principals, and if the business is not what it seems, don't let the outward glamor dissuade you from the reality that lies beneath. At some point, it may all fall apart, and you don't want to be caught in the fall. Instead, walk away. Perhaps find another job or take a vacation if you can afford one to give yourself some distance from what happened. And perhaps even tell the local police if you suspect fraud.

PART III:

UNDERSTANDING AND DEALING WITH THE SOCIOPATHIC LIAR

As discussed in the previous chapters, sociopaths can be described as having certain characteristics, which commonly include being outwardly charming and wearing a mask to conceal who they really are; being very goal-oriented and materialistic; having a lack of empathy; and having a lack of a conscience, so they don't feel any remorse or guilt for what they do, except when caught. They also have a great ability to lie, deceive, and manipulate to get to their goals, and if caught in a lie, they will often come up with still other explanations and excuses, so their lies can become bigger and bigger, while victims want to trust and believe and get caught up in these lies. They also have a desire for excitement and stimulation, and they don't take responsibility when something goes wrong, since their inclination is to blame others when convenient. Although, if something succeeds, they, of course, want the credit. All the while they look for vulnerable victims they can manipulate.

In some cases, sociopaths can end up in the criminal justice system, when their schemes lead them to commit crimes to get what they want, feeling they can readily break the rules. Or they may end up in the mental health system, when their behavior proves dysfunctional and leads to difficulties in relationships. But very often, their behavior leads them to be very successful in certain fields, where their traits contribute to them getting ahead, such as in sales and politics. Chapter 11 provides a summary of these topics.

As to why sociopaths do it, I did find one self-proclaimed sociopath who was drawn to do it because he felt empty and found it easier to tell lies to tell the truth, yet now he wanted help to overcome this. However, generally: successful sociopaths weren't interested in change, and the sociopaths I spoke to by phone or email described how they developed these characteristics in childhood. They also found that these behaviors, such

as being good at lying, manipulating others, and feeling no guilty contributed to their success, so they felt no reason to change. These themes are
described further in Chapter 12.

Finally, Chapter 13 deals with the question of what to do about dealing with a sociopathic liar. A first step is to recognize the major traits and
behaviors that characterize a sociopath, so you be careful in being caught
up into a relationship with that person, whether in a personal relationship
or in business. Remember that you will typically experience a honeymoon
phase, when the sociopath is very charming, wooing and courting you
into this relationship, but afterwards you will find the sociopath becomes
increasingly controlling and manipulative in seeking to get what he or she
wants. To this end, the chapter discusses the key traits and behaviors of
the sociopath to be wary of. Many individuals will have some of these
characteristics, so the key is to look for a combination of traits to identify
a person as a sociopath.

Then, if you feel you are dealing with a sociopath, the chapter describes
what to do. Check out your suspicions, such as noticing if the patterns of
behavior characteristic of a sociopath continue over time, to see if you
are accurate in your assessment. Additionally, consider gracefully getting
out of the relationship, cut your losses, and avoid being enticed into the
relationship. This chapter deals with these considerations in more detail.

CHAPTER 10:
UNDERSTANDING THE SOCIOPATHIC LIAR

As described in the previous chapters, sociopaths can be recognized by having certain characteristic traits, such as having no conscience, lacking emotions, wearing a mask concealing their lack of conscience and empathy, having a superficial charm, being determined to get what they want at any cost, and using an ability to manipulate and control to achieve their ends. They use lies to create a convincing narrative to appeal to prospective victims and pull them into their web, and they often build an extensive web of lies to protect and explain away previous lies if they feel threatened with being discovered. In the process, the victim can be devastated emotionally and financially. After they have no more need for their victims, sociopaths generally discard them and leave them behind, while they work on attracting other victims.

In personal relationships, this pattern of traits and behaviors often lead the sociopath to have a series of relationships with other partners, while lying about them to his or her significant other. In the business or work setting, this pattern can lead to the sociopath using a number of underhanded tactics to manipulate and control employees, business partners, customers, and clients, while taking advantage of them to gain power, prestige, and financial success.

Though their narratives differ in details, the many victims I spoke to described an experience of getting drawn in by an initial period of courting or recruiting. During this time, the sociopath charmed them in various ways, such as sharing similar interests, goals, and values, or offering just what the individual wanted, such as money, success, and power. A big difficulty for the victims is thinking these initial enticements in the courting/recruiting phase are true, since the sociopath appears to be who he or she claims, like a chameleon can blend into any setting by acting the part. Commonly, victims don't do much if anything to check out the sociopath in the beginning—or if they did check, they might have found that many things the sociopath told them do seem to check out, such as a website that appears legit, or the sociopath might have given them credible though vague information, so they can't do much checking. And often people don't have the time and energy to do much checking, feel it would be a violation of trust to do so, or want to believe what the sociopath tells them. As a result, the sociopath is able to explain away any negative information they encounter, such as a comment by a disgruntled former partner, customer, or client, by claiming they were seeking revenge because they lost out in some way, and so are not to be believed.

So there might be little you can do initially when you first meet someone or are presented with some opportunity, except to be initially cautious and get recommendations about the person from trusted friends and associates. Also, be alert in case any signs show up that the person or opportunity may not be what it seems. Unfortunately, sociopaths with schemes to take advantage of others can sometimes slip through, because people do have a tendency to trust others and respond to outward appearances. Most of the time this approach to living in society works; after all, you can't go around being skeptical of and checking out everyone. There's not enough time in the day, and you would be overly paranoid and could readily turn off others with your attitude of mistrust. But just be aware that sociopaths do take advantage of these cracks in the texture of everyday relationships and sometimes do get through, so just be aware—though not paranoid—when you do start to see signs and feel intuitively that something is wrong, because you could catch that bad apple that falls through.

In short, it's important to pay attention in the initial stages of a relationship or work or business opportunity or even after you get involved since there can be some warning signs that victims often overlook, though by themselves the individual traits or behaviors may belong to others who are not sociopaths, which is part of the problem of identifying successful sociopaths. They are experts at blending in and appearing like others, and people commonly have a propensity to trust, which is a basic building block of society. There has to be trust to keep a social group, organization, or community together, and the sociopath can easily play on that need and desire to trust by seeming to be trustworthy, when he or she is not. Still, with this caveat, some of the common warning signs are promises to do something or for something to happen, which are repeatedly changed or don't occur; repeated excuses or explanations to cover up any delays or changed plans; and an unwillingness to take responsibility or an effort to blame others when something goes wrong. I've included a more detailed list of how to recognize these warnings signs and what to do if you think someone is a sociopath in the following chapter.

More specifically, the signs to pay attention to are the following. Individual traits may mean nothing, since many people have these qualities, but taken together, these could be indicators that you are dealing with a sociopath. As described by Robert Hare, a psychologist and creator of the Psychopathy Checklist Test, the emotional and interpersonal traits include:

- being glib and superficial, egocentric and grandiose,
- having a lack of remorse or guilt,
- showing a lack of empathy,
- having shallow emotions,
- being deceitful and manipulative.

Their social behaviors include:

- being impulsive,
- having poor behavior controls,
- having a need for excitement,
- having a lack of responsibility.

They also commonly have early behavior problems and adult anti-social behavior,[140] though the successful sociopaths seem able to exercise the needed controls on their behavior so they fit in. In turn, it can be hard in the initial phases of meeting or working with a sociopath to know if they have these traits because of their ability to lie and deceive. As a result, as Robert Hare points out, "It is not always easy to tell whether an individual is being glib or sincere, particularly when we know little about the speaker."[141]

The Lack of Empathy and Feelings

Other characteristics reflected in these stories are their lack of empathy and shallow emotions, which contribute to the sociopath's ability to lie, deceive, manipulate, and control, since without feelings, they can readily lie, deceive, and hurt others by their actions without guilt or shame. However, this lack of empathy, feelings, and guilt may not be across the board, since some sociopaths, as illustrated in the stories we've read here, may have close family relationships and may care for and take responsibility for them. But they are able to compartmentalize, so they can be remorseless and relentless in business dealings, while still behaving ethically with family members and friends.

---

[140] Robert D. Hare, *Without Conscience: The Disturbing World of the Psychopaths Among Us*, p. 34.
[141] Ibid., p. 36.

By compartmentalizing, they can readily do whatever is necessary to get ahead, which might mean pushing aside or destroying anyone who gets in their way on the job, while then at home they can seem like loving, caring family members.

The Ability to Lie

These stories also illustrate the ability of the sociopaths to lie, beyond the everyday lies normal people use for many reasons, such as to be helpful or tactful, evade undesirable obligations, or present oneself in the best light. But sociopaths can use lies to create an even more inflated version of the self and build on an expanding web of lies, and they show no embarrassment or confusion on being caught in a lie, whereas others often apologize and confess. Instead, the sociopath may try to explain the lie away.

Then, too, the sociopaths can readily change their stories or rework their description of the facts to seem consistent with the lie. And for a time, the victim is apt to give the sociopath the benefit of the doubt, attributing the discrepancy or confusion to not hearing the sociopath correctly or perhaps mistaking the sociopath's meaning, not wanting to accuse the sociopath of lying. Moreover, sociopaths often show pride in their ability to lie and deceive well, as another example of their own superiority in that they are skilled at putting one over on others.

Seeking Satisfaction and Stimulation, Having a Lack of Responsibility

Likewise, the people interviewed told stories in which their partners, family members, and work associates exhibited other classic behaviors of sociopaths in their relations with others, such as doing things for immediate satisfaction, being outwardly cool, seeking constant stimulation, and showing a lack of responsibility. For example, Shirley was initially very cool and charming in getting Emily to advance her credit with promises of extensive additional work from clients, but after incurring a debt, Shirley was quick to come up with excuses for why she couldn't pay, while expressing appreciation for what Emily had done. As for Devon, he showed a lack of responsibility in turning to Virgil to bail him out by using his credit card to pay some of his debts and he avoided paying Virgil with a series of excuses about investors who were sending in their checks, which never arrived.

In Victor's case, he got Eric to do extensive work for him on scripts, until he was ultimately arrested and sent to prison for a boiler room fraud. This is an example of what Hare calls "trust mongers," people who use their professional position as a lawyer, doctor, investment counselor, or other professional, to take advantage to those who come to them for advice.[142] While some trust mongers take money from trust accounts or use their victims' payments to finance their high life—until the money runs out or their victims suspect them and they move on—others like Victor take advantage of their victim's enthusiasm to advance in an industry to get them to do work and then don't pay them. And sometimes trust mongers use the appearance of success in a high status position to entrap the victim, such as when Victor presented himself as a successful producer with powerful Hollywood connections through his well-known brother-in-law, when he, in fact,was divorced, had little contact with this brother-in-law, and was making money by running a boiler room scam.

The Vulnerability of Victims

This story also illustrates how victims can be vulnerable to be taken in by sociopaths, and get stuck in relationships they are reluctant to leave. But you can avoid the trap by being alert to the warning signs or get out once you are fully convinced you are dealing with a sociopath.

For example, sociopaths commonly lure victims by the initial charm and honeymoon phase, when sociopaths seem to know how to act to please the victim, based on sensing the victim's weaknesses and what he or she wants and needs. Then, they play off that assessment of their victims. If the victim is looking for a relationship, they share similar interests and values. Or to begin a business relationship, the sociopath can seem to have the very skills a person in business is seeking in an employee or partner. So you have to be careful when someone is mirroring your traits or echoing your wants and desires so perfectly. This could well be a sociopath luring you in. So take some time to pay attention before you become emotionally committed to a relationship.

Then, too, be careful about quickly trusting or believing someone who is very charming or offering what seems like a great job or business deal when you are new to a field. Take some time to check out what the person says to see if you can confirm it independently, and if you see discrepancies, that's a sign the person is not being honest.

The reason for being cautious is that sociopaths tend to be experts at lying, so they can tell a convincing though false story, and they are skilled at explaining away any inconsistencies and contradictions with more lies. Or they may be persuasive in claiming the victim was simply mistaken or probably misunderstood what they were saying. But often, the victim gives

---

[142] Ibid., p. 107.

the sociopath the benefit of the doubt, such as by attributing what is really an intentional lie to a misunderstanding or miscommunication. Or victims are too nice in trusting the sociopath and being receptive to believing what the sociopath tells them. So don't fall into their trap.

Another reason victims are vulnerable is because they find it hard to imagine that a sociopath could be trying to take advantage of them, when they are being open and honest themselves, expecting reciprocity in interpersonal relationships. That code of reciprocity is true for most relationships—you give something of yourself and it inspires the recipient to give back, unless you repeatedly give too much, then you come across as needy. By contrast, sociopaths use this natural desire of most people to want to help and contribute to take advantage of that spirit of altruism, so they may ask the victim for more and more, such as when a sociopathic son continually mooches off of his generous parents, or when a business associate repeatedly asks a co-worker or employee to do extra tasks for her.

If you notice any of those patterns, pull back from your willingness to be open and honest or repeatedly give more and more. You still have to be strategic in deciding what to do, but initially, just be aware of what is happening so you can determine what is best to do next.

Another caution is that when sociopaths seek to evade responsibility by denying they did something or blaming the victim, victims often think they must have made a mistake or did something wrong. They don't realize that the sociopath is lying to make their victims feel they must apologize or make amends. Once the victim does take the blame, or acts to set things right, this can set in motion a vicious cycle, whereby the sociopath feels he or she can easily use that "blame the victim" strategy again.

So if someone repeatedly seeks to blame you, when you feel you did nothing wrong, don't fall into that trap. If necessary, diplomatically act like you agree with the person who appears to be a sociopath, but otherwise, stand up for yourself or gracefully leave the situation.

Another problem for victims is thinking that they can change the sociopath—or that the sociopath wants to change and become a better person. To this end, the victim may excuse the past bad behavior, and often the sociopath is ready with reasons why he or she should be forgiven, such as an appeal to pity or call to help in overcoming some problem behavior. In some cases, sociopaths might make an appeal for understanding and help based on having a bad background growing up. Or the sociopath may promise that something won't happen again. So that's what often happens with sociopaths: they play upon the victim's gullibility and willingness to believe and trust that they want to change, but then they really don't; they just convince the victim to think they will or have done so.

Again, if you notice a pattern, be skeptical, because it may be a sociopath playing on your feelings of altruism and hope for a future that won't happen. So don't let such a situation go on once you realize how you are being victimized. Act to protect yourself, whatever fits in that situation, whether that means turning off your own emotional involvement in the relationship, looking for the best opportunity to break away, or leaving now.

Often victims do little until the end, especially in long-term personal relationships, since the sociopath's charm and confidence persuade the victim to continue to believe, and the sociopath's actions during the initial courtship and honeymoon phase contribute to the victim becoming more and more dependent on the sociopath. In a personal situation, the victim may feel very emotionally connected to the sociopath and not imagine that someone could be setting him up for a fall, because he would *never* do anything like that, while the victim of a sociopath in a business arrangement might feel her money is tied up in a venture or legal agreement and finds it difficult to get out.

CHAPTER 11:

WHY DO SOCIOPATHS DO IT?

While I found most self-admitted sociopaths or those identified as sociopaths by others elusive and not willing to talk to me, I found a few who shared their thoughts after I announced my research on several social media sites.

Fred: A Sociopath Seeking Help

One sociopath who contacted me was Fred, who introduced himself by acknowledging that he was sick, but was unsure where to get help. It was a rare admission for a sociopath, since most think their approach to life is fine and they admire their own ability to be charming, lie, manipulate, and control others to gain their trust. Still, Fred was interested in reaching out, though a little embarrassed at doing so. As he wrote:

"Hi there. I read on your page that you are an author writing a book about Sociopaths and are looking to interview people who are Sociopaths.

"Without giving much away, I think that I'm the biggest psycho/ sociopath and liar in history. If we talk, I'll explain why.

"I know that I'm sick and I'd like help, but don't know where to get it.

"I lack empathy of things and my brain is easier at coming up with lies than it is at telling the truth. I'm my own worst enemy; I'm a Frank Underwood (the diabolical political manipulator in *House of Cards)* in the humble guise of a Walter White (the chemist who becomes a drug dealer in *Breaking Bad)*; a John Galt (the entrepreneurial hero in Ayn Rand's novel *Atlas Shrugged* who confronts the corporate state), in the guise of Alyosha Karamazov (the younger brother in *The Brothers Karamazov* who is forgiving, kind and gives generously to the poor).

In other words, on the surface, Fred seems like a caring, giving individual, but this conceals an inner emptiness, because he lacks any emotional feelings and builds his life on lies.

Sociopaths Satisfied With Their Position in Life

The other sociopaths I spoke with generally were quite satisfied with their position in life, since they had become successful in their chosen field, although they wanted the cloak of anonymity by talking to me on the phone or via email. How did I know they were really sociopaths or that what they were telling me was the truth, since sociopaths are known for lying? Also, the individuals who spoke to me were not officially diagnosed, and they were speaking to me anonymously out of a fear of exposure. Those are valid questions, but I felt that if someone isn't a sociopath, why claim to be, since this is a stigmatized condition. Also, I found responses characteristic of what researchers have found that are the major motivations of diagnosed sociopaths/psychopaths.

In answer to my question of what led them to become sociopaths and why do they behave as they do, the half-dozen sociopaths I spoke to by phone or email said they knew early on in their childhood that they were different. When they were initially growing up and into their teenage years, friends and family members often noticed these differences and told them so, such as one upset mother who snapped at her teenage daughter after an argument, "You have no feelings. How can you be so calm about what just happened."

Other sociopaths talked about how they had feelings when they were very young, but closed them off because of something that happened while they were growing up. One man who said he initially sought out the warmth of his parents, but then he found his mother overly protective and domineering, while his father was usually reticent and emotionally distant. So rather than deal with his growing feelings of anger towards his mother and frustrations with his father, he closed down his emotions entirely. Then, he felt freer to do what he wanted, which included lying to get away with things he had done wrong or to obtain things he wanted.

Some were led into a pattern of lying, when they rebelled against their parents' repressive standards and did something they weren't supposed to. For instance, when she was fourteen and wanted to take riding lessons, Julie's middle class parents told her not to associate with classmate, Tamara, from a lower income single parent family, since they considered this association beneath their status. They also warned her not to go horseback riding, since they thought it unsafe and Julie could get hurt. But knowing they wouldn't approve, Julie spent several afternoons each week going horseback riding with Tamara, while telling her parents she was going to a school study hall to do homework. For several weeks, Julie was successful, until she strained her leg from falling off a horse and had to ask her parents to pick her up, since she couldn't bike home. Later, after promising not to lie again, Julie became better at lying when it was convenient, without any feeling of guilt. So, she continued to lie, and became better and better at it, while cultivating a reputation for being open and honest with her parents and family, but about things that didn't matter. Otherwise, she lied strategically when it served her purpose.

When asked the why question, the answers of the sociopaths were similar. Basically, they found that lying contributed to their success in getting what they wanted, and usually no one detected the lies. But if they did, they came up with other explanations, and commonly the person they lied to backed off. For example, Jeff commented:

> "I tell people what they want to hear, and if I have to give them false information or embellish something, I feel free to do it. For example, I have gotten jobs by telling people I have the experience in doing something. Then I learn what I need to, in order to do it, such as to lead a workshop on managing sales. I learned what I needed to put together a strong presentation. Later, I got references and more workshops to lead. What's important is that lying not only got me the gig, but then I showed I could actually do it, and do it very well."

The sociopaths also felt it helped to have no conscience or feelings about their lies, so they could lie more easily, but without showing signs of lying. They presented what they lied about as fact, and they commonly began with a grain of truth, which helped to give the lie more effectiveness. It seemed more realistic, though they conveniently turned some facts around to support the lie. For example, to get out of a debt he once promised to pay, Robert claimed he was now unsatisfied with a prototype which was delivered after a certain date, so he couldn't sell it as planned, although the delays were due to his changes in the original specs. And in classic sociopath style, he sought to blame the supplier when he himself was at fault for the delays. "So by lying I didn't have to pay anything," Robert said proudly.

Another reason the sociopaths gave for lying is that it seemed so easy to do so, because the victims were so ready to trust and believe them, and they felt no qualms about taking advantage of them. Rather, the victims were like a mark in the conartist's game; someone who could provide them with some benefit as long as they were useful, and they justified their actions on the grounds that the victims were stupid or losers to trust them. Or they characterized what they were doing as playing a game, which they won, and the victim lost. Another rationale which the business scammers used is that the victims were greedy or seeking an easy way to get money, so they were taking a risk on making the investment, and ultimately lost. So they had responsibility for lying about the benefits of a particular project to secure their investment.

The sociopaths were also able to readily come up with explanations, often in the form of new lies, to explain away any discrepancies or negatives should someone point them out. They attributed this to their ability to quickly come up with explanations. Should someone become overly critical, they felt they could easily move on and not engage with that person any more.

The sociopaths also felt as long as they gained, they didn't care what happened to the victim whose life or finances they disrupted or ruined. In their view, any upset the victim experienced was his or her own responsibility, and if a victim became too much of a problem, such as by contacting the police or filing for a civil case against them, they felt ready to leave.

Many sociopaths I spoke to expressed this same kind of pride in their lying and charm skills, such as Elena, an insurance sales rep, financial adviser, and stock broker, who had this to say:

"I've always been a natural sales person, since I'm very outgoing I know how to hook the client, by telling him what he wants to hear. I look for his hot buttons. Then, when needed I turn on the charm and may tell some stories to help seal the deal. It doesn't matter if they are literally true or not. If they work, I'm all for using them, and I do that with my boyfriends, too, so I can get them to do what I want. I've even created a whole invented resume that works in getting jobs and clients, and my friends and boyfriends don't really know who I am so I'm free to be who I want. So I know how to put on a good front and get away with it. And I'm proud I can do that, if I say so myself."

In sum, the sociopaths I spoke to provided the mirror image to the comments of the victims about dealing with a sociopath. Just as the victims found the sociopaths in their lives lied continuously and had no feelings or empathy for what they experienced as a victim, so the sociopaths acknowledged their lies and lack of feelings or concern for their victims. They also denied any responsibility for the problems caused and blamed their victims for falling for their charm, then falling into their traps. They viewed any harm they caused their victims due to their winning in a zero-sum game, which the victim lost. But, once the stakes became too high, and they perceived too much risk, they were ready to pull up their roots and move on to find a new victim. Or if necessary, they hoped to go back to family or friends to gain support for awhile, until they were ready to get back on their feet to play the game to win yet again.

CHAPTER 12:

HOW TO RECOGNIZE AND DEAL WITH THE SOCIOPATHIC LIAR

Given the potential for harm from a sociopath, who uses lies and other strategies to ensnare a victim, what should you do to avoid being trapped by a sociopath or how do you best deal with one who has entered your life? A lot of the options and strategies will depend on the nature of the relationship and what kind of power you have to change or end the relationship in the future. These same cautions can apply to dealing with someone with some sociopathic traits, as well as dealing with those who seek to control and manipulate you.

In a personal relationship some considerations will be how long the relationship has continued and whether you have entered into various agreements, such as renting or co-owning a house, having a business partnership, or lending someone a large sum of money. Having a child together can complicate matters further. Obviously, it is better to recognize early on that the person is a sociopath, so you can set up personal boundaries or end the relationship before getting in too deep. But if you cannot do so, figure out the best way to preserve your own emotional stability and sanity while negotiating your way out.

If you have a strictly business relationship, some considerations are the length of the relationship, whether the boss has power over you or a co-worker, if this is a customer or client, the amount of financial commitment involved, and what fallout to expect if you bring your feelings to the surface. For example, if the sociopath is your boss, some considerations might be how much you like your job, how much you need it or whether you can find another, and how well you can support yourself if you don't immediately find another job. Sometimes it can be better to grin and bear it, avoid rattling any cages, and try not to get emotionally upset by what is going on rather than making changes which could backfire on you

Whatever the situation, a first step is recognizing if you are dealing with a sociopath or likely candidate, because that person has a high number of the classic traits and behaviors that identify a sociopath. This first section will highlight the major characteristics to look for to identify the sociopath. The next section will consider what to do.

Recognize the Major Traits and Behaviors that Characterize a Sociopath

A first step to dealing with a sociopath is to recognize if the person has the major traits and behaviors that characterize one. Very few of these people will have come to the attention of the criminal justice or mental health system and very few will have engaged in voluntary psychological counseling, so few will have been officially diagnosed. Thus, you have to use your best judgment in determining if someone seems to fit the profile. Since a sociopath may appear outwardly to be like everyone else, pay attention to what they say or do to see if any hints appear either when you first meet or you see a pattern emerge over a period of time.

Since you can't often distinguish a sociopath in the beginning, be cautious in developing a relationship or entering into a business partnership or deal involving a serious amount of money, since those are the times sociopaths are most likely to appear—when there is an opportunity for sex, power, prestige, or money. These are key drivers for sociopaths who are especially concerned about gaining material success and putting on the necessary appearance to get there. While not everyone you meet with those very common drives will to be a sociopath, those are some key motivators. Look for other signs that suggest a person has those traits or behaviors.

Another consideration is how you have met this new person. It can be more assuring when you have met someone through personal or business connections, since you have more reassurance that the person has been vetted over time by others. Like everything in life, you can't be absolutely positive that a person you know hasn't been fooled by a charming sociopath; but at least your personal connection has had an ongoing relationship and perhaps positive feelings about this person. At one time, people used to meet through personal introductions and family and local community connections. Social institutions, like the church, school, and neighborhood, were stronger, so there were more controls in place. As a result, sociopaths, who now often move after they have victimized one or more people in a location, had less opportunity to look for vulnerable prey. Moreover, in the past, those with sociopathic characteristics were more likely to be restricted by community contacts, so they were less able to target and take advantage of the more vulnerable. These social influences are also why sociopaths are more common and comfortable in the anonymity of the city.

Now there are so many other ways of meeting new people, and many of these permit people to use aliases or handles, such as dating sites, hook-up apps, social media forums, virtual rooms online, and business networking events, so sociopaths can easily disguise who they are. All of these modern technology and network driven possibilities are available to be readily used by sociopaths in the guise of whoever they claim to be. And since sociopaths are masters of the mask and lie, they can easily fool many people with their claims.

Thus, be extra cautious when you meet someone through the social media or networking events, which permit people to easily present themselves as whoever they want to be. Sure, the meeting can lead to something which is glorious romantically or very profitable for business partners. But such meetings have also led to victims getting broken hearts and getting stripped of financial resources by sociopaths. As a result, in meeting anyone new, it might be good to start off slow, so you can check out if the person's stories continue to hang together and you don't discover any clues that the person isn't who he or she has claimed to be. For example, such clues might be messages delivered with the wrong name or address, improbable explanations, or repeated efforts to deny responsibility and blame someone else for something. With these caveats, here are the key traits and behaviors and what to look for, keeping in mind that individually, these characteristics may be the qualities of otherwise normal individuals.

A Summary of the Key Traits and Behaviors

As previously described, a sociopath has these key traits, as listed on the PCL:SV—Psychopathy Checklist: Screening Version developed by Hart and his colleagues.[143]

Key Traits and Behaviors of a Sociopath	
Interpersonal	**Affective**
Superficial	Lacks remorse
Grandiose	Lacks empathy
Deceitful	Doesn't accept responsibility
Lifestyle	**Antisocial**
Impulsive	Poor behavioral controls
Lacks goals	Adolescent antisocial behavior
Irresponsible	Adult antisocial behavior

---

[143] Babiak and Hare, p. 17.

Now let's turn this list of characteristics into qualities to notice yourself.

- **Recognize that sociopaths can easily look and act just like anyone else.**

There is no way to tell when you first meet someone if he or she is a sociopath, because they have a good ability to blend in, especially those who are very successful as entrepreneurs or in high positions in business, politics, and other organizations. As such, sociopaths are like wolves in sheep's clothing, as they move among everyone else who tend to go along to get along. Thus, don't be lulled when someone seems to be warm and friendly; until you get to know someone, their behavior could be just an act.

- **Pay attention when someone is very glib and charming.**

It is great when someone is very charismatic and articulate; they can be very stimulating and fun to be with, so enjoy talking and doing things with them. But also keep in mind that sociopaths commonly can be very smooth and slick, like a super salesman, politician, or an entrepreneur enticing you to invest in a new opportunity. While what someone is saying, selling, or trying to persuade you to do can be very real and good, exercise caution, so you take some time to get to know the person and check out them and their pitch.

- **If someone lacks remorse, empathy, or emotions—or seems insincere in showing feelings**

This lack of remorse or empathy is characteristic of a sociopath, who doesn't have a conscience or real feelings for others, although some sociopaths can compartmentalize, so they only show this lack of guilt or caring for others in a business setting, where getting ahead is everything. But commonly, sociopaths don't have these qualities of care and compassion with family, friends, and partners either. While you may easily be taken in on first meeting a sociopath, because of their skill in putting on a mask—where they appear to have feelings and pretend to be remorseful when caught doing something wrong—as you get to know a sociopath, you may get to see behind the mask. For example, you may see by their action that they really aren't sorry for something and don't really have any feelings themselves. The irony is they are good at sensing emotions in others, so they can know how to appeal to someone else and learn their vulnerabilities. Without feelings themselves, they can attack where they sense a weakness in someone else.

So pay attention to how someone shows their emotions and whether they seem sincere. For example, notice if someone is unusually calm and stoic, when others are showing strong feelings about something, like when something bad has happened to someone. The one major emotion that a sociopath might show is anger, such as when confronted by someone undermining his reputation or challenging her lies. But otherwise, a sociopath is often bloodless and uncaring, when not putting on a mask to charm a victim into a personal or business trap.

- **If someone tries to shirk responsibility and blame others, including you**
  Anyone may sometimes try to avoid getting blamed for something or to find someone else to blame to escape the consequences. A common example is the auto accident, when a driver says it wasn't my fault, or an individual brings in a lawyer to avoid responsibility or mitigate the damage. The difference is that a sociopath makes a pattern of evading responsibility and blaming others, which could be you. For instance, a client who can't afford to pay may suddenly claim some problem with the work, when there was none; an employee repeatedly excuses a poor performance by blaming someone else; or a boss yells at a team for not doing the job correctly, when he didn't clearly explain it. An occasional incident of evading responsibility and casting blame might not a sociopath make. But if it is a continual pattern, especially when combined with other characteristics of the sociopath, that's a warning sign to pay attention to.

- **If someone is very vague or general about details in their background**
  When you first meet someone in an ordinary social occasion or business networking event, you don't expect a lot of detail. But if things lead to a personal relationship, a possible business partnership, or hiring someone for important work, you'll want to know more. If someone deflects your questions or won't give you specific information you can check out and confirm, that's a time to be concerned.
  Moreover, you can do some independent checking, when you can, such as seeing if the person has a website or a LinkedIn or Facebook profile. If they don't have them, that could be a cause for concern, since most people and companies have these now. Likewise, you can easily check with a general online search. If someone claims success in a business, and if there is little or no online information about that person or company, or if the online information doesn't match what he or she has told you, that's cause for concern. You might also ask for specifics, such as the name of the person's business or the names of any clients for references. While many clients may be confidential, the person should have at least a few referrals, and when you check, ask for some specific things the person did to help you confirm that this is a real reference, not just a friend saying the person did a great job. All of this checking

may not help if a scammer sets up a credible-looking profile online and preps friends to support a story; but most of the time, a sociopath who moves from place to place after accumulating a few victims will not have the time or ability to do this.

- **Look for patterns of lying, big lies, contradictions, and efforts to explain away lies**
  You want to notice such patterns, since one of the core characteristics of a sociopath is being deceitful, which includes explicit lies, exaggerations, misrepresentations, and lies of omission, where a person doesn't tell you something that he or she should, or leads you to think something is true when it isn't. Even though people often don't think lies of omission are lies, they are, so if someone doesn't tell you something they should, explains away not telling you by claiming the information wasn't important, or say they forgot to tell you, any of those excuses could be a red flag. Certainly, an occasional omission might be a mistake, but if there is a pattern, that's a warning sign.

  Another concern to watch for is if the person repeatedly tells lies or exaggerates. Though there may be a germ of truth in the lie, the liar may twist that around or build on it to make false claims, such as claiming to know someone well after just a casual first meeting. Still another sign of lying to watch out for is where a person tries to explain away a lie after being caught lying or if the liar attacks you for wanting to know something. Another tactic is claiming you got information from people you shouldn't believe. Or a liar may use abject but insincere apologies for lying, such as claiming a reason was to protect you from knowing about a problem.

  Be wary too if someone claims you said, did, or agreed to something when you did not. While people can sometimes have differing memories of past events, if someone repeatedly contradicts your recollections, this is a form of "gaslighting" to get you to think you are forgetful or crazy for thinking things happened which did not. A good strategy here is to document anything you think is important or send a confirming email about your understanding, so you can refer to that document when a question about what was said or done comes up.

  Contradictions in factual information can also be an indication that someone is telling lies, so look for repeated contradictions, which suggest the liar is having trouble remembering what really is true. If you do point out a contradiction, commonly the liar may try to explain it away with a cover-up lie or try to convince you that he or she never said that in the past. But any such efforts to cover up or explain away past lies is another warning sign you may be dealing with a sociopathic liar.

- **If someone is being overly secretive**

Secrecy commonly goes hand in hand with lying. You should expect secrecy when others are working on a project or are pledged to hold something in confidence. But if you are in a close personal or business relationship and the person is being secretive about something that they shouldn't be, that's cause for concern, especially if they are giving you misinformation about what they are doing. Some of the possibilities include dating someone or leading a secret life if you are in a personal relationship, or being involved in activities outside the partnership, or covering up criminal activity in a business relationship.

Another sign of unwarranted secrecy can happen if you confront someone about secrets you discover. Instead of giving you a clear, sincere explanation, they create more stories or blame you for looking into something that isn't your business when you learned this information in a perfectly appropriate way, or they claim you are mistaken, when you are sure you are not. Such attempts to maintain or defend the secrecy can be a further warning of problems ahead.

- **If someone is especially focused on material gain or achieving a goal**

A reasonable concern with earning money and living a comfortable, even luxurious lifestyle can be fine, as can a dedication to achieving a goal. But if a person seems to have an obsessive concern with material gain or attaining a goal to the exclusion of having ordinary, caring human relationships, that can be a sign of sociopathy too.

- **Be concerned if someone is overly manipulative and controlling**

In some contexts, being manipulative and controlling can be beneficial, such as when someone is a CEO of a corporation or is a company owner running a business. Sometimes in a personal relationship it can be beneficial when someone takes charge at times, such as in a crisis, when a quick informed decision is necessary. But at other times, especially if being manipulative and controlling is part of a continuing pattern of behavior, this can be a red flag. Add a second red flag if this behavior is coupled with an attempt to isolate you from others, so the person can exercise even more control.

- **If someone is overly attentive in the beginning of a relationship, but then cools off and becomes distant.**

Sometimes a lot of personal attention in the beginning of any relationship can feel wonderful and it is typically part of a normal courtship and honeymoon period when everything is great. After a while, the relationship may shift into a caring, plateau phase, where you have become

comfortable with each other in a personal relationship or a business partnership. What is worrisome is if the other person is extreme in showering
attention on you in this honeymoon phase, since that can contribute to
your building a dependency on the other person. Alternatively, it is cause
for concern if the honeymoon phase is followed by a sudden drop off of
attention, since this frequently happens when the sociopath has gotten
what is to be gained from the relationship or has become bored and wants
to find more stimulation by moving on. This ending period can also be a
time of increased secrecy and lies to cover up other activities in the sociopath's life, which could be a danger sign that the sociopath is getting ready
to move on—and without you.

- **When someone has an inflated sense of themselves or of the things
  they are involved in**

  This inflated sense of self can be another sign of being a sociopath,
  because one of the sociopath's key traits is grandiosity, whereby they see
  themselves or what they are involved in as much bigger or more important
  than is the case. A normal sense of grandiosity might be reflected in someone having a grand vision or goal for doing something big, often followed
  by the necessary work to make it happen. By contrast, the sociopath has
  big dreams that aren't realistic, or he or she isn't willing to do the work
  needed to see the goal to fruition, since sociopaths tend to be impulsive,
  irresponsible, and lack follow-through.

- **If a person is frequently impulsive, drawn to stimulation, and readily
  breaks the rules**

  Often these traits of being impulsive, seeking stimulation, and
  breaking the rules can make someone seem exciting and fun to be
  around. It's like the attraction some women have to "bad boys" because
  they are so unpredictable adventurous, and thrilling to be around—
  like being at an amusement park. This same kind of rush that can lead
  men to test their limits in climbing mountains or engaging in extreme
  sports. But these same qualities can spell danger in a relationship, since
  it means after the honeymoon phase, a sociopath can get bored with you
  or a business partnership. Then, without the normal sense of responsibility, he or she may be eager to move on, leaving you or the business
  in the dust, or perhaps pushing you out in order to work with another
  partner. While it might be fun to go on a ride with someone with these
  traits, be cautious about entering into an ongoing relationship, because
  the fun times could end and you might find yourself on the losing end
  of a personal or business relationship, where the sociopath has chosen
  you as the next victim.

- **A losing combination**

  In sum, if you meet someone with a variety of these qualities, be cautious about getting more involved. Taken individually, any of these traits and behaviors might be expressed by anyone; but as they combine together into a pattern, be especially cautious. In particular, notice if any of these qualities are combined with repeated and extensive lying, because deceit is a central quality of the sociopath. It is a key strategy that sociopaths use to excuse or explain away other behaviors.

  For example, if you feel manipulated, the sociopath will commonly deny it or point out how he or she is trying to help. If you feel the other person is cold and callous, the sociopath may put on a warm, fuzzy mask to feign care and concern or will claim to have deep feelings, but doesn't show them. If someone has an inflated grandiose vision, he or she will give you reasons why it will work or claim others are excited about it, perhaps by using fabricated evidence or stories, too.

  In short, whenever you start to question or pull away from the sociopath's orbit, he or she will have a ready answer to pull you back in, if he or she is still interested in gaining something from you. Otherwise, the sociopath may respond to such doubts by cutting you off, acting defensively to protect their cover, or moving on.

  Thus, if you see a combination of these traits and behaviors, recognize that you might be dealing with a sociopath. Because sociopaths are so good at hiding and blending into their environment, they are social chameleons, and you may not be able to immediately recognize them. They are readily able to conceal themselves with the sociopath's mask and morph into being who they want to be or think you want them to be, so they are better able to prey on your vulnerabilities. Like the lion hiding in the bushes ready to pounce on a grazing antelope, they typically select for their victim the most vulnerable one who is grazing behind or alone. Likewise, a sociopath may look for a willing victim, cultivate a personal or business relationship, and strike to gain what he or she most wants—from sex, power, or material gain to excitement and fun—and later move on to the next. So pay attention and be cautious, so you don't become that victim.

Dealing with the Sociopathic Liar

What do you do if you suspect someone is a sociopath? Here are some guidelines, though there can be many possibilities of how to react in different situations. As a general rule, the best strategy is to simply get away.

- Check out your suspicions, whether they result from broken promises, suspected lies, repeated exaggerations, too many secrets, grandiose

claims, or gut-level feelings that someone is not to be believed or trusted.
There can be many ways to check, depending on the circumstances. One
method is asking a good friend who has met or knows this person about
his or her impressions; you may find he or she has similar concerns,
doesn't know the person as well as claimed, or knows others who have
suspicions, too. Another strategy is to check any facts of the suspected
sociopath or claimed affiliations on the Internet to see if they are true.
A third approach is to ask the suspected sociopath for a further explanation or more details, and if their explanation doesn't ring true or they
don't provide the detail you seek, this can help to confirm that the person is not to be trusted and, combined with other characteristic behaviors and traits, may be a sociopath.

- Don't let someone's position of authority or expertise lead you to put
  aside your gut-level suspicions. Your impressions, which derive from
  your unconscious intuition, will often be correct. Just treat your suspicions about a suspected sociopath as you would with anyone else that
  you have concerns about by asking for more information or doing further checking.
- Hold someone accountable if they repeatedly break promises, tell lies, or
  don't assume an expected responsibility. After someone doesn't keep a
  promise and is caught in a lie, or doesn't accept responsibility for something, a single mistake might be an ordinary mistake of humor error;
  or a single lie or failed responsibility might be due to a misunderstanding. In response, you might counter any broken promise, lie, and lack
  of responsibility by a reminder or discussion about what you expect, or
  you might remain silent and see if it happens again. The second time,
  you might still be forgiving, but monitor the situation to see if this is the
  beginning of a pattern. The third time, figure this is a likely sociopath
  who fits the pattern of breaking promises, lying, and evading responsibility; then act accordingly to break your ties as soon as you can.
- Talk to others you trust about the situation to get their support and sug-
  gestions on what to do. Others may have good advice, and if you expect
  to end a relationship, you may need their support to feel better about
  what you are doing.
- Once you believe someone is a sociopath—or shows the signs of being
  one from his or her traits or behaviors—the best approach is to end the
  relationship as soon as you can. Your goal should be to completely avoid
  the person or at least reduce any contact to as little as possible. If you
  can't take any actions immediately, make a strategic exit as soon as you
  can, such as if you are working for a sociopathic boss and need to find
  another job before you quit, or if you and a partner share a business or
  a child and you need to work out future arrangement. Do what you can
  to reduce your losses as much as possible when the relationship with

the sociopath ends, and then get out. And don't worry about hurting the sociopath's feelings; a sociopath has none. Moreover, once you have decided to get out, don't attempt to explain what you are doing or to try to work things out again, for such efforts will commonly lead to more empty promises and lies, so you are pulled back into the trap. So pull out and escape completely as best you can.

- If you have to remain in the relationship for a while, keep things running as smoothly and normally as possible, so the sociopath doesn't suspect you are seeking to jump ship. This way you are playing along to get along, so you can strategically decide the best way to extricate yourself from the relationship. It's a little like playing poker with a losing hand, where you minimize your losses while the game goes on, until you find a good time to ultimately leave the game.

- Don't think you can help the person to change, which is one trap that people in a long-term relationship with a sociopath often make. They think if they can talk to the person about what has been wrong in the relationship in the past and what they hope to change for the future, things will be different. But sociopaths generally don't want to change; instead, you will find that despite assurances to the contrary, things generally won't change, and the sociopath may use one of their last strategies by getting you to help and pity them. But if you accept, that makes you vulnerable to still more manipulations by the sociopath, who has found that the pity play works on you.

- Don't go along with any schemes a sociopath comes up with to take advantage of someone else, thinking you will be fine or that you can later shift the sociopath's behavior to be more rule-abiding. If you go along to help, you are enabling the sociopath to continue his or her sociopathic behavior. Worse, you may find that any arrangement to exploit someone else can easily be turned against you, such as when the sociopath decides you are no longer as desirable or useful, and he or she is ready to move on to the next victim. Moreover, you are unlikely to change any rule-breaking behavior to be more in keeping with the rules; instead, the sociopath is more likely to conceal such acts from you in the future or turn against you sooner. Plus, if any of these schemes involve evading laws, such as stealing property or information or scamming someone, you will become an accessory or even a co-conspirator in the crime.

- If this is a business relationship where money is involved, get everything documented in writing as best you can; if appropriate, write a final letter of your understanding of the agreement and any funds due, with a lawyer copied if possible, or ask a lawyer to write and send this letter. By taking these steps, you at least have written documents you might use later. Often a person receiving a letter or other end of relationship documents won't respond, which is even better, since by sending the letter, you can show you have tried to resolve things, if the matter should end up in court.

- If you are owed money, consider sending a letter where you offer to accept a partial payment, such as half, in return for resolving the matter amicably and ending any obligations and the relationship after that. You may get less than you want, but consider this an easy way to settle your losses and walk away from the relationship, rather than dealing with a prolonged battle to get your money through lawyers or going to court.

- Don't let the sociopath try to get back into your good graces by offering to reform if you give him or her another chance. This offer to change is another common ploy to continue the relationship, but after another honeymoon period, things may often go back to the way things were. Then, too, since sociopaths are so good at putting on the charm and manipulating others, this offer can be a way to set you up to further harm you, such as when a woman escaping domestic violence gets persuaded to go back or discuss the relationship, only to be attacked again—or even killed.

- If you cross paths with the sociopath again, such as in a social gathering, business networking, or other event, stay as far away as possible. Avoid any encounter if you can; try to avoid any eye contact by looking away once you notice the sociopath. If necessary, to be polite, just offer a brief hello and move away. If called into a conversation by a third party, try to find a gracious departure as soon as possible, and talk to the third party about the sociopath separately, at another time.

- Be cautious about getting involved in any third party relationships that may bring you into a relationship with the sociopath. Sometimes this third party may be someone you have met through the sociopath, and the sociopath and third party only have a casual connection, so there is no problem. But if the third party is acting as a go-between to bring you and the sociopath back together, that's a sign to stay away from both of them, since the sociopath is trying to manipulate both of you.

- Once you are out of the relationship, consider if there are any ways you can still profit from the relationship or learn from the experience for the future. Commonly, victims are only too glad to have the nightmare over. But there can be some things you can do to profit or gain from the experience later on. For example, if there has been extensive money involved in a business partnership or personal relationship, you might seek legal help to get back some of the money unjustly taken from you. If the sociopath has been involved in illegal activities, you might advise the appropriate legal authorities, unless this will jeopardize you, as someone who knew about and participated in these schemes, in which case talk to an attorney before you do anything. Another possibility is joining a support group for the victims of sociopaths to support your recovery, or become a spokesperson to warn others about what to look for and how to deal with the sociopaths they encounter. Then, too, you can take what you have learned from the experience to be more cautious in entering into new personal and business relationships, such as by checking out personal referrals or doing some checking before you make a major commitment. And, of course, look for the signs of a sociopath early in the relationship, so you avoid getting entrapped into that relationship in the future.

- In sum, once you suspect someone might be a sociopath, take some steps to confirm your suspicions. Then, if all the signs point to the person being a sociopath, take steps to end the relationship as soon and as gracefully as possible. As necessary, be careful in wrapping things up and cut your losses as much as possible. Avoid being enticed back into the relationship, which might repeat the honeymoon and victimization cycle and could even have worse results if renewing the relationship is a set up to harm you even more.